Dedication

For Skip, my husband, confidant, and best friend

Other Books by M. Kathryn Armistead, PhD

Nevertheless She Leads
Postcolonial Women's Leadership for the Church

(General Editors: HiRho Y. Park and M. Kathryn Armistead,
General Board of Higher Education and Ministry,
The United Methodist Church, 2020)

The Prophetic Voice and Making Peace

(General Editors: Matthew Charlton and M. Kathryn Armistead,
General Board of Higher Education and Ministry,
The United Methodist Church, 2016)

Conversations
*Leading United Methodist-related Schools,
Colleges, and Universities*

(General Editors: M. Kathryn Armistead and Melanie Overton,
General Board of Higher Education and Ministry,
The United Methodist Church, 2015)

Wesleyan Theology and Social Science
The Dance of Practical Divinity and Discovery

(General Editors: M. Kathryn Armistead, Brad Strawn, and Ron Wright,
Cambridge Scholars Press, 2010)

God-Images
In the Healing Process

(Fortress Press, 1995)

What readers are saying about
Live Faith. Shout Hope. Love One Another.

"Too many contemporary Christians think that faith is private, personal. Prodded by the Gospel of Matthew, Kathy Armistead shows that the Christian faith is public truth, good news announced and lived before all people. Here's lively, engaging encouragement for witness, for living our faith so that others can see and hear Christ through us. Kathy's book can help you to shine in a darkened world that needs Christ's light."

Will Willimon
Professor of the Practice of Christian Ministry, Duke Divinity School, United Methodist bishop, retired, author of Listeners Dare: Hearing God in the Sermon

"Kathy has a way of turning careful theological study into kitchen table conversation among friends. Small congregations take note. This is one of those resources written in love for your ministries."

Teresa J. Stewart
Author, speaker, consultant, and director of Small Church, Big God (SmallChurch.org)

"Kathy Armistead's gift of getting to the heart of a biblical text and applying it shine through in this meaningful study of the Gospel of Matthew. It is not only personally instructive and inspiring; it is helpful for small groups and classes who desire to deepen their understanding of what it means to be a disciple and to disciple others. Her experience and skill as a teacher and writer help to make simple and succinct that which is profound!"

Davis Chappell
Senior Pastor, Brentwood United Methodist Church, Brentwood, TN

"Kathy Armistead sounds like an internal, wise, affirming conscience talking to me about the practice of my faith. My own heart-voice recognizes her words as God-sent. She is deeply rooted in scripture and the Wesleyan tradition, but she is also connected to the common dailyness of living. May we be like the early Christians that she writes about…so that the way we live becomes an open invitation for others to experience the joy of life in Christ."

Dan Boone
President, Trevecca Nazarene University

"Here is a book that speaks to our shared experiences in a way that offers hope for a different future. I found the treatment of Jesus's words in Matthew to be informative and inspiring and a joy to absorb. As a therapist, editor, consultant, and pastor's wife, the author brings an intimate acquaintance with people whose stories illustrate profoundly the truths being discussed. These accounts from real people make it clear that God does enable people to live life to the full, love enemies, become generous, and reflect the joy God intends for all."

Richard Looney
United Methodist bishop, retired and author of The Fun of Being Looney

LIVE
Faith
SHOUT
Hope
LOVE
One Another

A Study Using Matthew's Gospel

M. Kathryn Armistead, PhD

Live Faith. Shout Hope. Love One Another.
A Study Using Matthew's Gospel

by M. Kathryn Armistead, PhD

©2022 M. Kathryn Armistead

books@marketsquarebooks.com
141 N. Martinwood Dr., Knoxville TN 37923

ISBN: 978-1-950899-63-0

Printed and Bound in the United States of America

Cover Illustration & Book Design
©2022 Market Square Publishing, LLC

Editor: Sheri Carder Hood
Post Production Editor: Ken Rochelle

All rights reserved. No part of this book may be reproduced in any manner without written permission except in the case of brief quotations included in critical articles and reviews. For information, please contact Market Square Publishing, LLC.

Scripture quotations used with permission from:

CEB
Scripture quotations from the COMMON ENGLISH BIBLE. © Copyright 2011 COMMON ENGLISH BIBLE. All rights reserved. Used by permission. (www.CommonEnglishBible.com).

ESV
The Holy Bible: English Standard Version
Scripture quotations marked "ESV" are taken from The Holy Bible: English Standard Version, copyright © 2001, Wheaton: Good News Publishers. Used by permission. All rights reserved.

KJV
Scriptures marked KJV are taken from the KING JAMES VERSION (KJV):
KING JAMES VERSION, public domain.

NKJV
Scriptures marked NKJV are taken from the NEW KING JAMES VERSION (NKJV): Scripture taken from the NEW KING JAMES VERSION®. Copyright© 1982 by Thomas Nelson, Inc. Used by permission. All rights reserved.

NRSV
New Revised Standard Version Bible, copyright © 1989 National Council of the Churches of Christ in the United States of America. Used by permission. All rights reserved worldwide.

NIV
Scriptures marked NIV are taken from the NEW INTERNATIONAL VERSION (NIV): Scripture taken from THE HOLY BIBLE, NEW INTERNATIONAL VERSION ®. Copyright ©1973, 1978, 1984, 2011 by Biblica, Inc.™. Used by permission of Zondervan.

Contents

Acknowledgments 1

Introduction 3
   Live Faith. Shout Hope. Love One Another. (Matt. 5:14-16)

Chapter One 19
   On Fire for God (Matt. 3:11)

Chapter Two 39
   Let Your "Yes" Mean "Yes" (Matt. 5:37)

Chapter Three 57
   Love Your Enemies (Matt. 5:44)

Chapter Four 75
   Be Generous to a Fault (Matt. 6:21)

Chapter Five 91
   Live Like There Is No Tomorrow (Matt. 6:25-27)

Chapter Six 109
   Forgive Seventy-Seven Times (Matt. 18:21-22)

Chapter Seven 123
   Make a Joyful Noise (Matt. 25:23)

About the Author 139

Notes 141

Acknowledgments

Publishing a book is a healthy exercise of a dedicated team walking the road to perfection, as John Wesley might say. I am especially grateful for the professionalism and dedication of this team, including publisher Kevin Slimp and my editor, Sheri Carder Hood.

I also thank the good Methodists of Middle Tennessee, especially the churches my husband and I served. You taught me, fanned the flames of my faith, inspired me, challenged me. Most of all you showed me that the church is still the best hope for our world despite our common human limitations and foibles.

Most of all, I am grateful for my husband, Skip, whose love, support, and encouragement have been instrumental in everything I do.

Introduction

Live Faith. Shout Hope. Love One Another.

You are the light of the world. A town built on a hill cannot be hidden. Neither do people light a lamp and put it under a bowl. Instead they put it on its stand, and it gives light to everyone in the house. In the same way, let your light shine before others, that they may see your good deeds and glorify your Father in heaven.

Matt. 5:14-16 (NIV)

Live Faith

It was Vacation Bible School time at Hilldale Church. As part of the program, the hundred-plus kids typically collected money for missions. The usual amount collected was about $500—a lot of money. This year, however, the pastor, my husband Skip, decided to ramp up the excitement. If they raised $2,000, he promised to shave his head. He offered his challenge and frankly thought he'd given the kids an impossible goal. He fantasized that his hair was safe. You can guess the rest of the story. The kids raised $2,734, far and above their goal. After worship the following Sunday, Skip had a barber in the congregation follow him outside (and a whole flock of kids and adults with cell phones). There in front of God and everyone, the barber did his work. Instantly, the event was uploaded onto Facebook and went viral.

That could have been the end of the story, but when Skip went about his routine—going to the YMCA, the grocery, the cleaners, and the hospital—startled and surprised folks took one look at him and asked: "What happened to you? Why are you bald?" Smiling, some asked: "Did the church finally make you pull out all your hair?" Never one to miss an opening, he gladly shared, "Our kids rose to the occasion and raised $2,734 for people in need." Shaving his head gave Skip and others a chance to witness about the good news of what was happening—how God was moving in their midst. It also gave everyone an opportunity to laugh with friends, neighbors, and even strangers.

Perhaps you've asked questions like these: How can I put my faith into action? What does it mean to live a Christian life? What difference can my faith make in everyday living? How can the Bible inspire me to lead a more rewarding life that can heal and renew the Earth? Or perhaps you just want to kick off your shoes and be at home. . .with God. If these questions speak to your heart, this book is for you.

Let's look around. In our world, there is a hunger for more—more money, more fame, more food, more followers, more likes, more stuff. We see people scrambling and climbing over each other, grasping and smacking down those who get in the way. We know that this hunger speaks to a deep spiritual hunger for God, but what can we do about it?

We also live in a culture where Christians are regularly misunderstood and misjudged. At times, Christians are often lumped together and broadly dismissed. Much of the world believes that, at best, Christians are mistaken—mistaken about how to live, mistaken about the possibilities for the peoples of the Earth, mistaken that peace will prevail. At worst, much of the world sees Christians as misguided, superstitious, anti-science, ignorant, and hypocritical. Even Christians grapple over how to share the Good News so that they don't turn off other people. Who wants to be seen as a "Church Lady"?[1]

So how can we live out our faith in our everyday lives?

Shout Hope

As the world gropes for answers, Christians say they have one. It's God. God is the answer. God brings hope. God is love. God cares for creation, and God is ever-present. But then comes the retort: "Where is the proof? Show me." Wrecked by disease, decimated by disaster and war, the world has good reason to ask: "Where is God—really? Where's the hope? Show me." One thing is for sure, the deeper our relationship with God, the more our lives will puzzle the world.

Christians always have hopeful, sometimes surprising, good news to share. If we live our faith every day in unexpected ways, people will see God's light in and through us. Then we can be ready to explain that we live like we do because of God. Christians offer authentic living, not gimmicks or tricks. Only God will satisfy our spiritual hunger pangs. Only God offers living water from God's everlasting wellspring of grace. As Christians, before we can provide hope and be a light that points to God, we first need to find God's light for ourselves. Perhaps a look at the earliest Christians will help.

In the early days of the church, people looked at Christians and questioned their behavior. The way they lived was at odds with the culture and often sparked curiosity, resentment, and even hatred. Since it could be dangerous to openly profess faith in Christ, people didn't necessarily go around talking about it. Christians had symbols—like that of a fish—that they shared amongst themselves to self-identify. Yet nasty rumors circulated and persisted. Weren't Christians the ones who feasted on human blood and flesh during the rite they called the "Eucharist"?

However, as the movement grew, Christians were spotted taking in babies who had been left to die. People saw them feeding the poor, treating enslaved people as equals, and being kind and generous to their persecutors. They even saw women in leadership roles. True, not all Christians did all these things, but they did enough to draw people to them.

One reason religious persecution stopped in some places during the Roman Empire was that there were just too many Christians to put in jail. When local city officials and important businesspeople and their families increasingly became a part of the Christian ranks, it was in no one's political or economic interest to ostracize or kill them. They were ordinary people living out their faith in ways that were incomprehensible to their neighbors. They were shouting hope in what others saw as a hopeless world.

There were also Christians in the Roman army, for example, the Theban Legion. They were called this because these soldiers were all conscripts from Thebias in Upper Egypt. As the story goes, all 6,600 were martyred in the year 286 at Aguanum (modern-day Saint-Maurice, Switzerland) where they had been quartered. The legion received orders to march to Gaul (France), but before leaving, they were also directed to make a sacrifice to the emperor, as was the custom. Because they were Christ-followers and worshiped God alone, these soldiers refused and only intensified their witness, consequently they were killed. Unfathomable to their generals, they chose Christ over Caesar. Years later (around 350), the bodies of the soldiers were discovered by Saint Theodore, the Bishop of Octudurm. The bishop built a basilica in their honor, and then in 515, the site became the center of a monastery, the remains of which are still visible.

In the early days of the church, many people became Christian because of what they saw Christians do. They saw lives full of hope, service, and giving—lives full of God's light. Yes, there are nuances in how people became Christian during those times. Some were baptized because the head of the house converted. Some were baptized because they were born into a Christian family. Some enslaved people were probably baptized because their masters became Christian. But the fact remains that when Christians professed their faith in Jesus and recognized Jesus as Lord, they sought to live out their faith through their daily behavior. They sought to shout hope as followers of Jesus in communities of faith—however understood—no matter what they called themselves, whether Christ-followers, God-fearers, members of the Way, or Christians.

Love One Another

During those early years, some Christians became hermits and lived apart from the world. For many, there is still a certain appeal for solitude and meditation, whether Christian or not. But many Christians believed then, and continue to believe now, that we are called upon to engage the world and be open to letting others who are different from ourselves engage us. This openness speaks to a love that motivates us to shine our light for others to see.

Deeds and Words

While Christians respond and react to their surroundings in different ways and with sometimes admittedly selfish motives, it does not mean that people don't pay attention to our actions. It also does not mean that we should witness only with our actions because, without an explanation, our lives serve only as testimony to ourselves. If someone does not know why we live as we do, they may miss the fullness of a relationship with Jesus Christ that is available to them too. We need words and deeds, just as Jesus used words and deeds, always pointing beyond self to God. We need words to interpret our actions because people won't naturally assume that we live for Christ.

Let me share an illustration. Two young men admired each other greatly in high school. One was a top debater and the other a noted athlete. Years later, when they reconnected, they found out they were both pastors.

One exclaimed, "When we were in school, I didn't realize that you were a Christian, but I sure wanted to be like you. I thought you were such a great guy, but I had no idea why."

The other replied, "I didn't know you were a Christian either. Bet our witness would have been more powerful if we'd known or teamed up somehow."

"Maybe," said the first, "if only you had told me."

"I was scared. I just believed that you'd figure it out, being a Christian, I mean. Guess I was wrong."

"Guess we both were."

When a person witnesses with their actions alone, they point only to themselves and not to God. People assume that these are, in and of themselves, just great people. They don't assume or connect that these persons are reflecting the greatness of God. If Jesus had only acted the way he did—healed the sick and taught with wise parables and ethical sayings—without telling us why he came, why he did what he did, and what was possible for us, we would think he was a great man who died long ago. We would not know what the Kingdom of God is or that it is possible for us too. But because Jesus told us who he was, he pointed us to God. He showed us what was possible for us. Sure, Jesus was a loving person; but if he hadn't told us why, we would have never figured out that what he had, we can have too—a personal relationship with God. To live out our faith, it takes words *and* deeds.

I was once shy talking about my faith until I went to work at our credit union. I loved working there. The services were outstanding and affordable, and the philosophy about being an owner, not just a customer, really impressed me. Being part of the credit union was a great thing, and I wanted all my friends to know about it. So, I started inviting people to join. Then I thought, if I could share how great the credit union is or even how scrumptious a coworker's fudge recipe is, surely, I can share how amazing God is and explain what God has done for me. I thought about it and crafted a couple of sentences to share should the occasion arise, and I rehearsed it. I wrote something like: "God is a big part of my life. God has done more for me than I can begin to tell you. We also have a friendly church if you want to check it out." Or, when someone was new in town, I'd ask them if they had found a church yet. If they were looking, I'd tell them we had a great one.

I admit the first time or two, I was nervous. How would they react? I thought to myself, "Telling someone how to get free checking isn't hard, so telling someone to check out our church shouldn't be either." And it got progressively easier to share. I wanted to live my faith out loud. I wanted to shine my light, not hide it under a bushel.

Create Communities that Defy Expectations

Being a Christian means that we invite others into the community of Christ, and, for them to accept, we must be people who they want to be around. Nobody likes pessimistic, critical, stingy, or unwelcoming people. So, our faith communities must offer hospitality and genuinely and generously care for others.

Not long ago, my husband and I were visiting different churches, trying to find a place where we felt at home and could serve. We heard good music and good preaching, and for the most part, the people were friendly. But we left many churches feeling like all hope was gone from the world. We didn't leave lifted up, and in one place, I felt like someone had beaten me over the head. When we invite someone to church, they should see Christ through the congregation's actions toward them. That's the kind of church I want. Don't you?

When Christ is fully present in our life together and the Kingdom of God comes into fruition in the life of individuals and communities, there has to be evidence of that reality in the way people act. It's not make-believe or wishful thinking. Christ should be so obviously present in our behavior that people should say, "Wow, God is truly present." And each one of us needs to be so invested and dedicated to prayer, Bible study, and service that when we get together, we produce shock waves or, as Leonard Sweet might say, "faithquakes."[2] This responsibility falls on each of us to do our part; it's not only up to the pastor, paid staff, or lay leaders. The atmosphere of a church reflects all the people there. No one can say magic words, and poof, God appears. God is not like a genie who materializes out of thin air; in fact, we should remember that God is already present because God is omnipresent. It is up to each of us to be so in tune with God that when we gather together, we produce a beautiful symphony of Spirit-filled worship and praise so people can experience a foretaste of the glory divine.

As Christ-followers, we must be aware of what we

communicate to others who might not be a part of the faith community. While we might be misunderstood, it's worth the risk, and the needs are so great. Prayer is obviously something we can do. Every church has saints and prayer warriors who can help and who probably are already helping—because God never leaves God's self without a witness anywhere.

Surprised by Joy

When we let our light shine for God—when we live faith, shout hope, and love others—we count on God to use a person's curiosity or surprise to notice. As C. S. Lewis writes of his own conversion in his book, *Surprised by Joy,* we want people to be surprised by joy. A person's decision to follow Christ must be a free choice. It can't be manipulated or coerced. A person's choice comes from being increasingly attuned to God's prevenient grace, God's wooing, but our lives can serve to make others sit up and notice.

I know that in today's world many people are beaten down (literally and figuratively) by family, jobs, and maybe life in general. It can be difficult for them to exude joy, hope, or love when they hurt so badly. But enduring hardship doesn't mean you have to turn inward or away from God.

Early in our ministry, my husband and I became acquainted with two women. They were both well into their sixties. They had gone to school together, gotten married about the same time, and had a child about the same time. So far, their lives were going as expected. Then one night, the kids decided to ride home together from a ball game. They weren't far from where they lived when a drunk driver broadsided the car. Both kids were killed. And, of course, both mothers were devastated.

As time passed, one woman turned increasingly to God while the other persistently kept turning away. The first woman lived a productive life and became a saint in our church. She said that despite the tragedy of losing her child, she never lost sight of God's hope in her life for which she was grateful. This woman had such a warm and joyful spirit. She was kind and generous, the type of person people wanted to be around. The other woman's life, however, took a different turn. She drifted from her friends and church family and then from God. By the time we met her, she was cold and bitter. She had withdrawn into herself and rarely left her house. When we visited her, she was unwelcoming and seemingly uncaring. It was quite sad, and I've never forgotten. Each woman was a powerful witness, the first to emulate and the second to avoid as a cautionary tale.

God's Presence

How can we shine our light in witness so others will see God and seek a relationship with God for themselves? Unlike my husband Skip, most of us are probably unwilling to shave our heads, no matter how much attention it draws to God. But Jesus lived the kind of life that people noticed. I'm sure Jesus recognized the fact that crowds have an insatiable appetite for spectacle, which continually ups the ante and temptation for gimmicks. People paid attention to Jesus because of what he did, what he taught, who he healed, who he ate with, who followed him, and who he said he was. To be sure, some people—particularly those with something to lose or those heavily invested elsewhere—may not have liked what they saw and heard. Yet, despite the risks, God calls us to live like Jesus. So how are we to act so that God is glorified, the church fulfills its mission, and others understand and join in witness? In our information-saturated world, what should we do? How can we compete when there is so much noise in the air?

No worries, God has already given us the most powerful tool on earth: God's presence. There is no more powerful story of the joy of God's presence as we find in the book of Philippians. Toward the end of his ministry, the apostle Paul wrote to his beloved church. At the time of his letter, he was imprisoned, bound by chains, waiting for, what turned out to be, his death sentence. Yet, he is joyful. He says: "Rejoice in the Lord always. Again I will say, rejoice! Let your gentleness be known to all men. The Lord is at hand" (Philippians 4:4-5, NKJV). Philippians is known as the "Epistle of Joy," because of Paul's attitude despite his suffering. Paul preached joy and he lived it.

Paul rejoiced in every circumstance and found joy amidst his hardship. In his writings, he advocated that we do that too. In Philippians we see that Paul had every reason to be discontented and upset by the world's standards, yet his zeal for God, his joy in Christ never wavered.

We too can have this joy and the hope and love it brings. We can start by opening the Bible and learning the basics about who God is and what it's like to be God's people. And the book of Matthew can be a good place to begin.

How to Use This Book

This book uses passages from the Gospel of Matthew to guide us and frame our conversation. This is fitting because, for centuries, the church used Matthew to teach the basics of the faith. These fundamentals can help us put our faith into practice as Jesus intended.

This book contains seven chapters. Each chapter focuses on one aspect of Christian living taken from the Gospel of Matthew, so that we can fully live a life that lives faith, shouts hope, and loves others. At the end of the chapter, there are reflection questions. These are meant to be a reality check and are suitable for individual or group study. These reflection questions are designed to help you reach the next level in living out your faith so that when others see you, perhaps they will also get a glimpse of Jesus. In addition, there are suggestions how you can "bring it home." This is what you can do to put your thoughts and heartfelt insights into practice and make them part of your daily living.

Reflection Questions

1. Share a time when you felt joy.

2. Share three things you hope will come out of this study?

3. In what ways are you living the life you believe that God wants for you?

4. Share a time when you felt close to God. Who was there? What happened?

Bringing It Home

1. Light a candle each time you begin this study. Let it remind you of God's presence and Christ's love for you.

2. Every time you pick up this book to read, consider beginning your study by praying this prayer by Saint Richard of Chichester (1197–1253), which is based on the parables from Matthew and Luke.

Thanks be to thee,

my Lord Jesus Christ,

for all the benefits which

thou hast given me,

for all the pains and insults

which thou hast borne for me.

O most merciful Redeemer,

Friend and Brother,

may I know thee more clearly,

love thee more dearly,

and follow thee more nearly.

CHAPTER ONE
On Fire for God

He will baptize you with the Holy Spirit and fire.

Matt. 3:11 (NRSV)

God's Fire Propels Us

The people of Jerusalem and around Judea came to see John the Baptist. Here was a man making quite a stir—a prophet, a holy man, a person on fire for God. Matthew's gospel tells us that many took his words seriously and were baptized. While we may not know much about John the Baptist, this much we know for certain: John captured people's attention; yet, he knew his limits. After all, he could only baptize with water. Someone was coming who would baptize with the fire of the Holy Spirit—Jesus.

With these expectations, the Gospel of Matthew sets the stage for Jesus's ministry. And Jesus does not disappoint. When John later baptizes Jesus, a dove descends, and a voice from heaven says, "This is my Son, the Beloved, with whom I am well pleased" (Matt. 3:17, NRSV).

People saw John and must have wondered why his words touched them so. What was it about this man?

John wore odd clothes and ate strange food. His words harkened back to prophets of old, yet they rang true to the crowds that gathered. But John knew his role was to prepare the way for Jesus. That was his purpose. John was on fire for God. His goal was not to call attention to himself but to point others to the one who could give them God's fire—Jesus.

Methodists love this quote from their founder, John Wesley: "I set myself on fire and people come to watch me burn." So, the story goes, this is how Wesley answered when asked why people came to hear him preach. While scholars say that Wesley really didn't say this, the quote is apocryphal nonetheless, and it makes a good point about living a life as a beacon for God. People need to see the fire of God in us.

God's fire propels us to act. It enables us to live faith, shout hope, and love others. It burns away all that doesn't matter, purifying our motives and making our actions transparent, so that when others see us, they can also see a reflection of God's glory, God's fire, the *shekinah*. (See 2 Chron. 7:1-3.)

Available to All

Being on fire for God is a gift from God, made available to all at our baptism. Living a life on fire for God means that God is our consuming passion; God is our first priority. But with all the religious strife and name-calling in our society, God has gotten a bad rap, because some people do bad things in God's name. So unless we continually seek to know who God is, are grounded in scripture, and are part of a community of faith to keep us accountable, we can be tempted and easily led astray. We all can be. As much as we may want to point to the true God, we may find ourselves pointing to something else or someone less.

After Jesus was baptized, Matthew describes how Jesus was "led up by the Spirit into the wilderness to be tempted" (Matt. 4:1, ESV). What happened there? We might say that Jesus faced his demons. Grounded in scripture, along with the practices of prayer and fasting, Jesus drew strength and prevailed. Then the first thing he does afterward? He finds others to be part of his inner circle—a community of disciples. With no illusions about what is to come, Jesus begins his ministry. We too must be willing to be led by the Spirit even into a wilderness.

Christians on fire for God must put away their selfish desires for personal fame and power. The world will find this inexplicable and counter-cultural. Why would anyone work so hard and take none of the credit? We also need to put aside illusions and childish images that we may have about God. Putting aside "childish things" (I Cor. 13:11) means we are better able to enter into the fullness of a relationship with God, not as we want God to be but as who God really is, at least as much as anyone can truly understand the great I AM.

What does this mean? Many people, especially in the United States, grow up believing God is some kind of super-sized Santa. What is tragic is when we seek to mature in our faith, we may not have a viable alternative. We cling to the security of what we think we know instead of letting God lead us into the mysterious unknown. If God isn't like Santa—loving, jolly, supreme gift-giver, and record-keeper—then who is God? People on fire for God don't have all the answers, but they will walk with us, pointing us toward an ever-deepening relationship with God so that one day we may see "face to face" (I Cor. 13:12).

A Bigger God

During my days as a Christian counselor, I had a client who was angry at God. As she explained it, she had good reason. God had taken her father away from her when she was twelve. Her reasoning as a child was that if God could do anything, God could save her dad if he (and God was a "he" in her mind) really wanted. But her dad died, so God either did not care or was cruel. In either case, she didn't want anything to do with God, and yet, she was afraid not to believe. She just wanted God to conform to her wishes and needs. As for therapy, she was ambivalent toward me and the counseling process much of the time because she saw me as God's representative.

You might say that her ambivalence even led her to marry a minister. The marriage alternated between periods of heated engagement and mutual aloofness. She found herself competing for her husband's attention with this same God. Because she was the pastor's spouse, her husband wanted her to keep up appearances and go to church so she could be seen by the congregants as his adoring wife. However, she was confused and feared confronting her emotions each time she went. Consequently, she took every opportunity to stay away from church.

Feeling stuck in a cycle of seeking God, then pushing God away and, not coincidently, seeking closeness with her husband and then pushing him away, she spiraled down into depression. She finally decided that she was going to have to come to terms with her feelings, so she made an appointment with me.

She was in conflict. She believed in God but didn't like the God she believed in. She couldn't imagine a God of grace. So, she fought God—at least the God she thought she knew. The only way she knew to relate to God was by being angry with God, which ultimately led her into depression, which manifested itself in all her relationships. Yet, she kept coming to counseling. Once she had the courage to face her ambivalence, she began to turn the corner and consider that God might be different than she imagined. God might be more than what she originally believed.

Or consider this story. Alan[3] lived down the street from me growing up. He moved away when he was in middle school, and I didn't see him for eight or nine years.

As it turned out, we went to the same university; and one day, I saw him briefly across campus, and we waved hello. Then years after we graduated, he came home to visit his grandparents, and we had a chance to get reacquainted.

When I knew him as a kid, Alan didn't really have any friends. One night, he prayed to God to make his teddy bear come alive, so his teddy bear would be his best friend forever. He thought, "God can do anything, so why not make my teddy bear alive?" The next morning, he woke up fully expecting his teddy bear to greet him, but it just sat in the corner next to the train set. Being a bright kid, he thought that maybe he didn't pray hard enough. So that night, he prayed again, "Oh, please, God, make my teddy bear come alive." But his teddy bear just sat looking at him blankly. Alan thought that maybe he wasn't praying the right way, or maybe if he was extra good, God would make his teddy bear come alive. But try as he would, his teddy bear did not come alive.

Alan decided that if God was all-powerful, God could do anything God wanted. God was also supposed to be loving, at least that's what he heard at church. So, either God was not all-powerful, in which case he wasn't worth bothering with, or God didn't really love him, in which case he wasn't worth bothering with. In either case, Alan decided in his ten-year-old heart that God wasn't real.

But there is more to Alan's story. As an adult, he began thinking about God and his teddy bear. As a grown-up (and even as a child), he knew that teddy bears never come alive, so he thought there must be something wrong with his logic. Then he remembered. While he was praying every night for his teddy bear to come alive, his father suddenly announced, without giving any reasons, that they were going to move. When they moved, Alan found himself in a neighborhood filled with boys about his age. His dad put up a basketball hoop in the backyard, and every day after school, four or five kids played there—in his own backyard. Here he was up in his room praying for his one teddy bear to come alive when God had provided the opportunity for him to have five new friends. God did answer his prayer, just not the way he wanted. "God is," Alan said, "much bigger, much grander, much more generous than I could imagine. I was limited in what I wanted, but God had better plans for me. I've wasted years not getting to know this awesome God."

My client's and Alan's limited image of God not only hindered their relationship with God, but prevented them from experiencing fruitful and significant relationships with other people. It wasn't until Alan realized that God is much bigger than he ever imagined that he found new meaning and purpose in his life.

What if I'm Afraid to Be on Fire for God?

I think it's normal to be a little afraid of giving yourself over to be "on fire for God." When I was young, my mother had a book about Christian martyrs. One afternoon, I finally mustered my courage and opened its pages, but I quickly closed it again because of the gruesome pictures. "Is that what God expects me to do too?" The thought made me shudder. What if God asks too much of me? I wrestled with what I would do if confronted with a choice between God and living. Perhaps you've had similar thoughts. What would you do?

Learning about the sacrifices made by those martyrs made me reluctant to give my entire heart to God. What if God asked me to give up my life? What if God wanted me to die for God? Many people have and still do today. Martyrdom is real. While I confess that it's still hard for me, I've decided a couple of things. First, the God I imagined demanding my life "or else" was not God. God doesn't desert us, especially in our time of need. My childhood God was a construct of who I thought God was, given my limited knowledge and experience. Our God does not want us to die for God. God died for us. Rather, God wants us to live and live for God. God wants us to be witnesses and serve as God's hands and feet in the world. God doesn't create martyrs; hateful people do.

We need not be afraid to live for God.

Seek Others to Walk with Us

This book is about how to live a life that lights a path to God's kingdom in the here and now. That is what results from living faith, shouting hope, and loving others, and, like Jesus, we don't have to do this alone. And it is not about what we do to "climb up" or "reach up to" God. Even that language should make us think something doesn't ring true—"up," "down," or "out"—these words are meaningless when describing God. When we are on fire for God, we're not striving to appease God. Being on fire for God means that the fire of God's presence is in us and flows through us. Being on fire for God is about living so that God's kingdom is in plain sight for all to see. It shows others a reflection of who God is and what it means to have a relationship with God. But be aware, there's a good chance that God is more and different from what you've been taught or seen on TV, Facebook, Twitter, or whatever social app is trending.

Billy[4] was bright and had a full ride to do whatever he chose at the university. However, this school also required attendance at chapel services. It was a church-affiliated school, so no big surprise. Billy grew up in a conservative Christian home. His parents were fine people who only wanted what was best for their son. Billy went to chapel like everyone else, but something was simmering inside him. He felt that God was stifling him. God had so many requirements and rules, and Billy was ready to shuck them all.

Then he took biology, and the professor explained evolution. It seemed to make sense, but he knew his parents wouldn't approve of him believing in it. He got an "A" and then moved on to the 201 class—zoology. By the time he was a senior, Billy had mastered as much about genetics as any undergrad, and he understood evolution's basic mechanics of natural selection. But the more he learned in his science classes, the less room there was for God until, finally, he announced that he was an atheist. It was not a hard decision for him—or so he said. God was X; science was Y; therefore, X cannot be Y. Oil and water, God and science, do not mix.

I'm not sure if he ever told his parents. He knew his decision would devastate them, because he suspected that his mother secretly hoped he'd become a missionary. No chance of that now. For whatever reason, Billy decided that God had to go. The sad thing was, however, that Billy only needed to let go of his childhood image of God. That perception of God wasn't big enough anyway. That God was confining and too limiting. God is so much more, but Billy cut off his relationship with God and any faith community, so he'll never know how much more there is.

In college, I was a zoology and chemistry major. By the time I graduated, I had also mastered as much about genetics as any undergrad, and I knew the principles of evolution. But my studies only deepened my convictions about God. It was exciting to better understand how people talk about the universe. Understanding science made my image of God bigger. For me, science could never eliminate the need for God. Rather, science only illuminates how limited our human insight is and, by any comparison, how grand God is. I wanted to live with God's kingdom in plain view, and the more I learned, the more I saw the need for others to help me. We're not better or smarter than Billy, but we can seek out people of faith to walk beside us—something he did not do.

People on Fire for God Can Guide Us

If we want to know the truth about someone, we don't listen to the gossip of others. We find out for ourselves. And if we really want to succeed, we enlist some trusted friends looking for the same things we are. For instance, if you want to travel to another country, you need things like a guide, a map, a passport, and encouragement to keep moving forward. That's what people who are on fire for God do. They act as beacons to guide us through dark terrain. That's why I'm always on the lookout for people on fire for God. What about you?

Do you know someone whose inner light burns so bright that it shows others the way? You may have seen pictures of the holy family, saints, or angels with halos around their heads. One reason that artists depict them this way is because it is a way to show how, through their lives, the light of God burned.

Jesus was God in the flesh, but he was also fully human. Matthew's gospel is clear on this point. Jesus was tempted. Given the expanse of the universe and our teeny planet in one of the millions of galaxies, it seems absurd when we try to wrap our minds around God becoming like us. How is that even possible? The best I can do is imagine that Jesus was filled to the brim with God's light, so much so that it overflowed. God's love and power must have gushed forth and spilled out all around him. God's light must have burned so brightly that people had to avert their eyes. With Jesus around, all who encountered him could see and feel God, the Great Light.

Surely the fire of God that shone in Jesus came with a deep intellect, an open heart, and a tremendous sense of humor. There must have been so much faith, joy, and love crammed into his human body that it had to explode in a resurrection. Even death could not contain him. It certainly cannot contain God's love for us.

You know the story of Moses and the burning bush, the bush that burned but was not consumed; in other words, it didn't burn up. Jesus must have been like that bush too. He burned for God but was not consumed. In fact, Jesus made it clear that the zeal he had for God, the life God has to offer, is available to us too. There is no fear that God will use us up and then discard us. God does not use up people for God's purpose; God lights a fire that cannot be quenched, a fire that shows us—and others—the way into God's kingdom.

People on Fire for God Illumine God's Reality

People on fire for God illuminate God's reality and can be identified by how they treat others. God's reality is God's kingdom, and it is characterized by blessedness even in the midst of adversity (Matt. 5). As the book of Galatians tells us, the Spirit of God results in fruitfulness—the fruit of the Spirit—joy, peace, patience, kindness, gentleness, goodness, faithfulness, and self-control (Gal. 5:22). If you want to know if someone is on fire for God, look closely at their behavior. Do they love others? Are they kind? Are they faithful? Are they joyful? Do they love their enemies? Do they love the truth? Do they unselfishly serve others? Do they shine a light on God's reality?

By now, you may be thinking that you could never be on fire for God. Who can live so faithfully like that all the time? Or you might think that only saints can. But underneath it all, never fear; the fire is burning. God does not desert us. Perhaps your passion for God has dwindled to a few dying embers. Do you need someone to help fan the flames? Perhaps you just have to position yourself so that God can rekindle the fire of God's love in you.

You may have heard this story before, but it bears repeating. A traveling preacher was lost in the wilderness. He saw a light ahead and stopped at the lone cabin on that snowy evening. A man welcomed him and showed him great hospitality. After a fine but simple meal, the two talked by the fire. The preacher thanked the man and said, "You have been generous and kind to me tonight. If it wasn't for you, I'm not sure where I would have slept or if I would have eaten. Let me do something for you in return. There's a revival at Piney Church tomorrow. Come and worship with your fellow Christians." The man said,

"Thank you. Your visit has been a real blessing, but I can worship out here by myself. I don't need other Christians to help me do that." Then the wise preacher took a stick and stuck it into the fire. When he found a single burning coal, he drew it out on the hearth, away from the rest of the fire. Neither man spoke. They just watched as the coal slowly went out. The man got the message.

God never meant for us to be alone. In God's reality, we cooperate by sharing gifts and talents for the common good to transform the world in light of God's will. After all, not all are teachers, not all are artists, not all are woodworkers, not all are theologians, and certainly, not all are plumbers. Some of us can contribute a lot, and some can contribute only a little. By ourselves, we can only sustain our fire for God for so long; but together, we can help bring in the kingdom on Earth as it is in heaven.

Sal[5] was on fire for God until her husband died. Having been happily married for twenty years, she suffered from grief and loss. Those times when Sal thought she would just give up, Christian friends were there to support her. Then Sal lost her job, and she wondered why God was punishing her. Her savings were dwindling, and for the first time in her life, Sal desperately needed help. She had always been the one to help others, but now she needed to be on the receiving end. She felt as though she was all alone.

But Sal continued to go to church, and she even began

tithing her unemployment checks. She threw herself on God's mercy and studied the Bible even more. Since she had more time on her hands, she decided that she might as well do some volunteering. The more she attuned herself to God, the more she began to feel God's presence. Still, she knew her flame was flickering and ready to go out any minute, so she decided to join a small group at church. Slowly, hope returned, and her soul revived. She could feel the warmth of love and concern from those around her.

Did her story have a happy ending? She could never put the loss of her husband behind her, but she was grateful for the time she did have with him. She found another job, although it paid less money. She blossomed with the fruit of the Spirit; her faith matured. When her fire was all but out, she leaned on others' fire for God, and eventually, her spirit was rekindled by the fire of God's love through Christian friends.

When we experience seasons of trouble or hardship or when our fires are doused by tragedy, those are the times we not only need God more, but we also need Christian friends to fan the flames of God's presence. That is God's reality.

People on Fire for God Warm Us with God's Love

Fire can bring warmth and a controlled blaze can provide comfort. People on fire for God emanate God's love, and we are drawn to them. Jack[6] was a Vietnam vet suffering from PTSD (Post-Traumatic Stress Syndrome).

He didn't go to church because he didn't feel worthy to be in God's house. Who was he to God? Jack's life was a mess and he knew it. Worse, he made his family's life unbearable. He had thought about suicide for years before he finally decided to go through with it. Jack found his gun that he kept locked away, cleaned it, and bought ammunition. He carefully planned to take his own life while his wife was at church on Sunday. He didn't want her to walk in and interrupt him. And most important, he didn't want her to get hurt.

That Sunday, Jack's wife went to church as usual, and Jack put his plan into action. He even took steps to minimize the clean-up that would be needed afterward. He held the gun to his temple, ready to pull the trigger. He took a deep breath, ready, holding steady. All of a sudden, he stopped. At that moment, Jack decided to give God one more chance. He dropped to his knees and mouthed the only prayer he knew, the one his mother had taught him long ago. "Now, I lay me down to sleep." He laughed. Then he cried, and cried some more—a lot more. Now what? He called a friend, who led him to confide in some other close Christian friends. One of those friends had just come home from the Walk to Emmaus, a seventy-two-hour Christian program sponsored by the Upper Room.[7] Jack knew many in his church had participated in the Walk to Emmaus and returned "a new person" with renewed zeal for the faith, but more than that, Jack's friend told him that he would experience the love of God like he never had before.

Perhaps this was the chance he had been waiting for. Jack balked, but still, his friend persisted. Finally, the friend overcame all Jack's objections, and Jack went on the next Walk. And there it happened. Everything his friend said was true. For the first time in a long time, Jack felt God's love. He felt it through the selfless service of others—people who didn't even know him. Jack felt it as he learned new things about the faith, and he felt it in the powerful worship.

Jack came home a new man. His PTSD was more manageable, and his emotional outbursts were less severe. But his sense of hopelessness was gone and gone for good. Jack knew that it would be too easy for him to backslide, so he asked his pastor if he could do something that he'd wanted to do for a long time—organize the church to send care packages to soldiers in Afghanistan and Iraq. His pastor was thrilled, Jack began this new ministry, and the church mailed boxes all over the world.

Jack knew God was nudging him to do something more daring: share his witness with the church. Many people knew him, but no one understood what he'd been through. On a Sunday morning, Jack spoke to an astonished congregation. He shared about his PTSD, his anger toward God, and his attempted suicide. With great dignity, he explained how he experienced the love of God on that Emmaus weekend. Many were moved to tears, especially some of the other veterans in the congregation. As a result of Jack's testimony, he and a few other veterans began reaching out to younger soldiers returning home or who were on leave. God only knows how many lives Jack saved.

As if that weren't enough, Jack's persona also changed. Instead of a gruff, older man who put people off, he became a kind, loving father-figure, and people were drawn to his warmth—or rather, God's love exuding through him. Jack was on fire for God. Sparked by the fire of others, Jack found his light and was now burning for God as he shared his light.

A Walk to Emmaus prayer begins: "Come Holy Spirit. Kindle in us the fire of your love." When we are on fire for God, we are not being braggarts or offering ourselves up as a gimmicky spectacle. We are seeking to live wholeheartedly for God. We are seeking first the kingdom. As people look at us and scratch their heads about how we live, God will utilize us to show who God truly is. And because of our light and our fire, people will find the Greater Light of Christ and feel the warmth of God's love.

Baptized with Fire

When we are baptized, God pours out his Spirit on us. God says to us, as God said to Jesus, "You are my beloved, a child of God" (Matt. 3:17). You may have heard it said, as I have, that baptism is our initiation into the church. If that is all we think it is, we are cheating ourselves. Baptism is more than the formal acknowledgment that we believe in Jesus Christ. We are baptized with water and the fire of the Holy Spirit.

Perhaps you remember your baptism. I remember mine. I was only about four years old, but I will never forget how it felt to be washed and purified. I felt so clean that night when I went to bed that I was afraid I'd do something wrong and mess it all up the next day. Of course, the feeling faded, but the thought that I was God's child no matter what and that God was with me forever never went away.

Perhaps like you, I have experienced the fire of God's love many times. And while I need help rekindling my fire from time to time, I know that the fire of God's love never fails and that God always has witnesses burning brightly if we only take time to look.

Reflection Questions

1. Who was your best friend growing up?

2. Who is someone you admire and want to be like?

3. Reflect on your baptism story.

4. Share a time when you met someone who was on fire for their team, their job, their organization, God.

5. What did you think God was like when you were five years old? How have your views changed?

Bringing It Home

1. Prayerfully make a list of ten things you are grateful for.

2. Call or visit a friend you haven't seen in a while and reconnect.

3. Find something that "lights your fire," something that is exciting to you and share it with a friend. Or if you are using this book as a group study, share your passion with the group next week.

4. Connect with someone who might need to experience the warmth of God's fire through you?

CHAPTER TWO
Let Your "Yes" Mean "Yes"

Let your "yes" mean "yes," and your "no" mean "no."

Matt. 5:37 (CEB)

Standing on God's Promises

Beginning in Matthew 5, Jesus lays out teachings about how to live the life of a disciple. Here we find the beatitudes and many other well-known passages, such as the admonition that Jesus's followers are to be the salt of the earth and light of the world. One prescription for living that doesn't get its due is Matthew 5:37. This is where Jesus says, "Let your 'yes' mean 'yes,' and your 'no' mean 'no.'" The context of this statement involves taking oaths and giving testimony—giving your word, truth-telling—but I also understand this passage to mean: Don't go back on your word, because keeping your word demonstrates your integrity. In so doing, we can reflect God's steadfast lovingkindness—God's promise to be ever present, ever faithful. As the embodiment of God's Word, Jesus was faithful in all things. And while we humans will falter and fail, we can always stand on God's promises, God's Word.

Peter Storey is a man of integrity, a man of his word, a person whose life is defined by living faithfully, often at great cost to himself and his family. Before I say more, there are some things you need to know about Peter. Peter's pastoral ministry was largely spent in inner-city churches, most notably in District Six in Cape Town and the Central Methodist Mission in Johannesburg, South Africa. Here he spent many years opposing the infamous apartheid government and its oppressive, racist policies, particularly during the forced removals of people of color. Later, as a denominational bishop and ecumenical leader in the Johannesburg/Soweto area, he played a significant national role in South Africa's anti-apartheid struggle. He also served as chaplain to Nelson Mandela and other political prisoners on the notorious Robben Island where he narrowly escaped his own assassination. When the apartheid regime was put on trial, he and Bishop Desmond Tutu were witnesses-in-chief. He continues to fight for justice by preaching and lecturing around the world. Further, Peter founded South Africa's Life Line, a telephone-based crisis-intervention service, and Gunfree South Africa, the nation's anti-gun movement.[8]

During the apartheid years, Peter and his family were hounded and under constant police surveillance. He paid a high price for keeping his commitments to God and promoting human dignity and racial equality. Many reasonable people asked him why he continued the fight for justice. You can be sure that Peter's "yes" is "yes" and his "no" is "no."

In South Africa during apartheid, the government decided to increase its military to quell resistance, so they instituted a draft. Many young men unwillingly went to support the government and a cause they didn't believe in—except a few who refused to sign up or serve. One of these young men who refused was Peter's son. He, like his father, had made promises to God. Peter's son and one of his friends, who also decided not to serve, agreed they would face the consequences together—being put on trial with the certainty of prison. The friend's trial was first, and, not surprisingly, he was sentenced. Then it was Peter's son's turn. The night before the trial, the church gathered for prayer, asking for a miracle. As the trial began, the government's case was overwhelming. Peter and his wife, Elizabeth, were about to give up hope when the judge suddenly and unexpectedly called the court to adjourn. Everyone went home, and the trial never reconvened. That was it—a miracle.

To this day, Peter doesn't know why the court proceedings abruptly came to a halt, but he suspects that it may have had something to do with him. Perhaps the trial was meant to send Peter the message to back off. If that was the intent, it didn't work, and it didn't weaken Peter's or his family's commitment to God. Through it all, Peter stood on God's promise to be a very present help in times of trouble (Psalm 46).

There is power when you stand on God's promises and your promises to God.

God's Commitment to Us

When we give our word to God, it's serious. Joshua 24:15 (KJV) says:

> *And if it seems evil unto you to serve the Lord, choose you this day whom ye will serve; whether the gods which your fathers served that were on the other side of the flood, or the gods of the Amorites, in whose land ye dwell: but as for me and my house, we will serve the Lord.*

In the Bible, a commitment with God is called a covenant. The word "covenant" comes from the Hebrew word *berît,* which means "to cut." A covenant was a legally binding obligation. Today we would call it a contract. In biblical times, however, people literally "cut" a covenant, which could be done a number of ways. When the parties were equal in status, both might cut their palm and then shake hands, letting their blood mingle. Other times, animals were sacrificed by cutting them in half, and one person—typically the person of lower status—would say something like, "So may it be done to me if I do not keep this agreement." When a king made a covenant with his vassal, the vassal would walk between the bloody animals, knowing this would be his fate should he break his side of the agreement.

God's covenants with people are usually unilateral.

God alone determines the terms and conditions; humans choose whether or not to accept them—with a "yes" or a "no." The first covenant God makes in the Bible is with Noah, and it extends to all. The terms are recorded in Genesis 9:8-17. Here God promises to all creation that "never again" will God destroy human beings or the earth by flood. The King James Version says, "And I will establish my covenant with you; neither shall all flesh be cut off any more by the waters of a flood; neither shall there any more be a flood to destroy the earth" (Gen. 9:11, KJV).

In a typical Hebrew play on words, God cuts a covenant, promising not to cut off life. Then after the flood, God sets God's "bow" in the sky as a token for us to remember—a reminder and a promise—a rainbow. While God sets all the terms for this contract, God does not ask for any reciprocal action from Noah. God made an unconditional contract with all creation in this act. What is so startling is that God asks for nothing in return. There is no "other side" of the agreement. God, in effect, cuts a covenant with himself alone.

Yet, despite being Ruler of the Universe, God does not hesitate to take the part of a servant. To be sure, we see this in the life, death, and resurrection of Jesus. But we can also see it in Genesis 15 in God's covenant with Abram. As I mentioned above, when a king and a vassal made a covenant, it was the vassal—the weaker, the one with less power—who walked between the animal carcasses, saying, in effect, "So may it be done to me if I don't keep this covenant." In Genesis 15, it is God who "walked" between. We see this beginning with Genesis 15:17. When making the covenant, God caused a deep sleep to come upon Abram. While he slept, the sun went down, and then it was God who passed between the carcasses in the form of a burning lamp. God took Abram's place in the ritual, bearing both God's part and Abram's part of the covenant. This demonstrates God's love and commitment—God promises—to us.

Our Commitment to God

Still, it seems like some of our standards aren't what they used to be. Not long ago, an active church member was defined as someone who attended church every Sunday and participated beyond that. Today, an active church member is defined as someone who attends worship one or two times a month, and the typical in-person worship attendance is one-half to one-third of the membership.[9]

When people join a church, they make commitments in terms of their time, gifts, talents, service, and witness. How are you doing with your commitments to God? For example, let me put it this way, how many people have you brought to Christ through your service and witness—ever?

One a Month

My pastor colleague Bob[10] had a young woman in his congregation who more than lived up to her commitments. It started when she was in high school. Her small church was having its annual revival that week. During the altar call at that first service, the preacher challenged people to bring someone with them the next night. In fact, the church already had cards with the names and addresses of people who were willing to be invited. Sally[11] felt especially convicted and took a card. To her relief and dismay, she recognized the name on the card. It was someone she saw every day at school. It was Stephanie. Never having done this before, Sally asked a friend sitting in the next pew to accompany her when she invited Stephanie to the worship service.

The next day, when Sally bumped into Stephanie at school, Sally hesitated. She rationalized that her friend wasn't there for support, and they could go to Stephanie's house later anyway. Then it was past supper and nearly time for the service to start. Sally lost her nerve. When she went to church that night, she wrote "not interested" on the card and gave it back to Bob. But in the wee hours of the morning, Bob's phone rang. It was Sally. "Something wrong?" "No, but I have to see you now. I did something terrible." Bob didn't think that Sally could do anything that terrible, so he said, "How about you come by the house before school tomorrow? Can it wait that long?" "Yes," said Sally, "I'll see you tomorrow, early." Bob could tell something was up.

At 6:30 a.m. sharp, Sally knocked on the back door, and Bob was there to greet her. Neither one had slept well that night. "What's up?" said Bob. And Sally let loose with the whole story—how she broke her promise to God, how she chickened out, how sorry she was, but could she have a second chance? Then she took a deep breath. Bob took it all in and looked at her with kind eyes, retrieved the card, and handed it back to Sally. "See you tonight?" he said. "You bet," she said and ran out the door.

It was a long day at school, and Sally felt her confidence ebbing; but true to her word, after supper, Sally took her friend, and they drove to Stephanie's house. They parked across the street and sat and sat. Sally finally knew that if she didn't go now, she'd never go. So, she and her friend ran up and banged on the storm door. Stephanie's mom quickly appeared and smiled curiously at the two kids standing on the porch. She could tell the girls were uncomfortable. In a higher-than-normal pitch, Sally asked, "Is Stephanie here?" Stephanie's mom nodded and said, "Sure, no problem. Would you like to come in for a glass of lemonade?" "No!" Sally blurted out.

Stephanie heard Sally's voice and came running. "Hi, Sally!"

Sally could not contain herself, "God loves you, and I love you. Want to go to church with us tonight?" There, she had said it.

Stephanie gathered her thoughts, looked at her mom, and said, "I've wanted to go for a long time. I'm so glad you asked. Would you give me a couple of minutes to get ready?"

When they arrived at church, the congregation was singing the final hymn. "We almost missed it!" said Sally breathlessly. All three ran up the aisle where Stephanie gave her life to Christ.

Afterward, Sally was elated. "Despite the fact that I almost blew it in so many ways, God used me. Even me." She later told Bob that if she'd known how good she would feel, she would have done this a long time ago. "But, Brother Bob," she added, "If I don't do this again right away, I'll get nervous, and odds are that I won't invite anyone again. So, I'm going to bring someone to Christ every day for the rest of my life."

In his quiet way, Bob said, "Why not one a month?"

"Okay, one a month."

Bob thought the conversation was over, but he was wrong. There were two more nights of revival, and as good as her word, Sally brought people both nights, and she walked with them as they went down the aisle and accepted Jesus as their savior.

From that time forward, while she was in high school, Sally brought people to church, and at least once a month, one of those persons gave their life to Christ. Then she went away to college.

One afternoon as Bob was working on his sermon, the phone rang. It was a pastor from the town where Sally attended college. He asked, "Who is this girl? Who is this girl that keeps bringing people to our church altar month after month?" And Bob filled him in. "Gee," said the pastor, "I've never seen anything like it. I knew there had to be some explanation."

Years went by, and Bob didn't hear from Sally. Then one day, he got the call, the one all pastors look forward to receiving. "Brother Bob, I'm getting married. Will you do the ceremony?" It was Sally.

Bob says that Sally was the most radiant bride he'd ever seen on her wedding day. As he looked out over the congregation, the church was packed. It was filled with people Sally had brought to Christ. As he pronounced them "husband and wife," Sally turned and whispered in Bob's ear, "One a month."

Sally keeps her covenant with God and shines her light for all to see. How about you?

Over and over, God makes good on God's word, and if we want to be a shining reflection of God in this world, we need to do the same. This is what it means to live a life of faith, hope, and love.

Be Not Afraid

Joseph was a poor carpenter (Matthew 13:54-54), although the Greek word for carpenter can also be translated as stonemason. In any case, he had a humble position in the social hierarchy, yet he was also a descendant of King David, the most revered and beloved king of Israel. As we learn in the Bible, Joseph was engaged to be married to Mary, and while we don't know much about Joseph, we do know how engagements worked at that time.

An engagement was a legally binding contract, or covenant, between two families. It could not be broken without serious consequences or unless there were dire circumstances. Often an engagement included a financial transaction, which might include land, livestock, and jewelry. Like much of the Greco-Roman world, the Jews in the New Testament celebrated marriage in ways reflecting ancient customs. The heads of the family—the fathers—typically arranged marriages, which were sometimes used as part of a broader business agreement. The bride brought her a dowry into the marriage, which often remained her property even if her husband divorced her. In addition, the groom might pay a bride price to the father of the bride, although this was not understood as the bride being purchased or sold into marriage. Many believe that this practice was also meant to protect the woman in case of divorce.

Like today, attitudes toward marriage varied and interpretation of marriage laws differed. We do not know the exact arrangements between Joseph's and Mary's families, but in all cases, the bride was to be a virgin. The penalty for being pregnant outside of marriage or by a man who was not the husband called for the stoning of the woman and the man as well.

As we read in Matthew 1:19, Joseph was a righteous man. When he discovered that Mary was pregnant, he decided to "dismiss her quietly." To be sure, Joseph was righteous; but being a righteous man, at least in the eyes of his peers, meant that he should follow the law. Clearly, in this case, he did not. Joseph's righteousness was not defined as blind obedience to the law or conformity to social norms. Rather his righteousness was foremost a right relationship with God. He was committed to keeping covenant with God. Our righteousness is not blind obedience, although sometimes that may be necessary. But even our obedience stems from and is firmly rooted in our relationship with God as shown in the example of Jesus Christ.

By keeping his promise to marry Mary, Joseph was doing three radical things. First, he was admitting that he was the father; and if not that, second, he was assuming legal responsibility for the child. This commitment meant that Jesus would be his son with all the rights and privileges afforded a natural-born son. Third, in the eyes of the community, Joseph was accepting shame on his family—hardly the way anyone would want to begin a marriage.

What caused Joseph to live out his righteousness by this course of action? God sent an angel who spoke to him in a dream. "Joseph, son of David, do not be afraid to take Mary as your wife, for the child conceived in her is from the Holy Spirit" (Matt. 1:20, NRSV). What is often overlooked is that, although Joseph had already decided to be merciful to Mary, he likely made that decision, at least in part, out of fear, perhaps for himself, perhaps for Mary, perhaps for the child's future. Like any of us, he must have asked, "What will people think? What am I getting myself and my family into? Where does my love for Mary stop and my family obligations begin?" Perhaps it was just that simple. His love for Mary was the only important consideration. One thing is for sure, God's love for Mary and Joseph was paramount as was God's desire to give Jesus loving parents. Even so, Joseph had a choice and he chose not to be afraid. That can be our choice too.

What if We Don't Know or Can't Keep Our Commitments?

What do we do when we want to keep our promise to God, but we don't know how or can't fulfill our commitment? Life is complicated. Sometimes right and wrong have blurry edges. It's not a question of which path we take, but where is the path? How can we see the way forward when the road is obscured by impenetrable fog? Have you ever been in that situation? Perhaps you can't find the right path because you've been blinded by ambition, pride, wishful thinking, or, like Joseph, fear, anxiety, and even love.

Martin[12] loved The University of Tennessee Volunteers. He never missed a football game and surrounded himself with orange paraphernalia, the team color. In fact, his apartment looked like it was decorated for a perpetual pep rally. When he and Penny decided to get married, Penny converted to being a Vols fan, which wasn't too bad. After all, she loved him. She was not happy when Martin decided they needed to plan their wedding around the university football schedule, but she acquiesced. She didn't say anything when Martin insisted that the colors of the bridal party attire be orange and white. And she didn't say anything when, on the day of the wedding, the game went long, and Martin insisted they delay the ceremony until it was over.

Penny was a strong woman of faith, but when she finally figured out that Martin was obsessed with Tennessee football and that she would always take a backseat, she threw up her hands. She loved him, but what should she do? She had already said "yes." They were married. She wanted to keep her vow of "till death do us part," but it was getting harder to overlook Martin's preoccupation. She feared ending up old and alone. She prayed and talked to Christian friends, but she felt silly telling them about Martin and his uncontrollable passion. . .for the Vols. It hurt her pride to think that Martin paid for season tickets rather than the honeymoon they'd originally planned.

Penny studied her Bible, looking for answers, and felt God's prompting—or was it just her own inclinations? One thing she knew for sure: God was with her. Finally, she realized that it took two people to make a marriage work, and from her point of view, she was the only one committed to this marriage. Love may have blinded her and she might have been afraid of making a wrong choice, but when the fog cleared, she filed for divorce.

Humans have limits. God understands that. God is not blinded by love for us. God truly sees, and that's why we don't have to be afraid. God's love illuminates the truth, and God's grace helps us choose to do our part. Commitment is a two-way street. A promise to God involves both God and us. But with God, we know that God is faithful and will keep God's word. We don't have to worry that God will break God's covenant with us. Our job is to keep up our side. And even if we don't or can't, God's steadfast lovingkindness never fails. The good news is that even when we can't fulfill our promises, God is there to help us find the path so we may continue walking with God.

Perhaps you say God spoke to Joseph through a dream. Yes, God did, but Joseph was open to hearing God's message and recognized the voice of God because of his deep relationship with God. What if we, unlike Joseph, don't receive a direct word from God in a dream, Bible study, or anything else? What if we're stuck not knowing which way to go? Then we do as the great theologian and reformer Martin Luther advised:

> *Be a sinner and sin boldly, but believe and rejoice in Christ even more boldly. For he is victorious over sin, death, and the world. As long as we are here, we have*

> *to sin. This life is not the dwelling place of righteousness but, as Peter says, we look for a new heaven and a new earth in which righteousness dwells. . . . Pray boldly— you too are a mighty sinner.*[13]

In other words, in this world, we will err and make wrong choices. That's just the way it is. When in doubt about the way God is leading you to go, do not be afraid. Pray boldly, then take a bold step. God will be with you regardless. So walk with confidence. Be not afraid.

Conclusion

God honors his covenant with us. Letting our "yes" be "yes" will lead to a life that reflects God's steadfast faithfulness. The key is to maintain our relationship with God. It is only through our relationship with God that our "yes" can be "yes," and our "no" can be "no." As the sheep of Jesus's flock, we know God's voice; we know it because of our long-time familiarity with God. We can be people of integrity and keep our commitments to God only because we know the God to whom we make these promises. We know what God expects. God expects us to "do justice, love kindness, and to walk humbly with our God" (Micah 6:8). When we can't or don't, God is ready to forgive and help—on this, we can depend. It is God's commitment. God's "yes" to us is everlasting and the personification of God's "Yes" is Jesus.[14]

Reflection Questions

1. What does it mean for a person's word to be their bond?

2. Reflect on a time when you or someone you know made a promise that they could not keep.

3. Share a time what you had to say "no" or God said "no" to something you asked.

4. Name a life-changing decision that you made.

5. How is God reaching out to you? What do you need from God now?

6. How can you be a more effective witness to help others better understand who God is?

7. Is God asking you to say "yes" to something?

Bringing It Home

1. There are many lists of God's promises posted on the Internet. Find a promise that is especially meaningful to you. Write it on a note card and place it where you can look at it every day this week. Here are some examples to get you started: Deuteronomy 4:29; Psalm 121; I Chronicles 16:34; Matthew 6:33; 1 Peter 1:14.

2. Take a picture or draw or find an image that represents God's love for you. It might be a picture of nature, family, or something or someone else. Share it with a friend or loved one.

3. Think of a promise that you might want or need to make to God.

CHAPTER THREE
Love Your Enemies

"But I say to you, love your enemies. . ."

Matt. 5:44 (NKJV)

Who Is Our Enemy?

Loving one's enemies is a part of living a life that's full of God's hope and love. But how badly do you have to dislike someone before they become your enemy? Surely, the people I don't like at first sight are not my enemies. They are just people who look irritating, saying a lot more about me than about them. And surely, an enemy is not the same as a competitor. When I ran track, I didn't think the runners in adjacent lanes were my enemies, even though we all wanted to finish first. We were competitors. Enemies are also not the same as adversaries. You may hold an opposing viewpoint or block me in some way, but that alone doesn't make you my enemy. And enemies aren't necessarily critics, especially if they only want your attention. When we think of an enemy, we imagine someone who hates, someone from whom you will get no quarter, no mercy, no slack.

While I hope you don't have enemies, Sigmund Freud thought, by virtue of standing for principles, mature individuals would, by definition, have enemies. He regarded enemies as part and parcel of what it meant to be civilized people who contribute to the social order. Whatever you may think of Freud and while we might define enemies by our feelings toward them or their feelings toward us, when Jesus talks about enemies in his Sermon on the Mount, he is talking about our behavior toward others. People may proclaim themselves to be our enemies, but we don't have to reciprocate their stance toward us. Jesus doesn't call us to like our enemies, but he does tell us that we should do right by them despite their ill will toward us. Jesus says:

> *You have heard that it was said, "You shall love your neighbor and hate your enemy." But I say to you, love your enemies and pray for those who persecute you, so that you may be sons of your Father who is in heaven. For he makes his sun rise on the evil and on the good, and sends rain on the just and on the unjust. For if you love those who love you, what reward do you have? Do not even the tax collectors do the same? And if you greet only your brothers, what more are you doing than others? Do not even the Gentiles do the same? You therefore must be perfect, as your heavenly Father is perfect.*
>
> **Matt. 5:43-48 (ESV)**

Being True by Doing Right by Our Enemies

The Matthew volume of the Anchor Bible series translates these verses differently and in a way that gives another perspective:

> *You have heard that it was said, "You shall love your neighbor and hate your enemy," but I tell you to love your enemies and pray for those who misuse you. In this way you will become sons of your heavenly Father, who causes the sun to rise upon both good and evil men, and sends rain to just and unjust alike. If you love only those who love you, what reward have you? Do not the tax gatherers do the same? And if you greet only your brethren, what extra are you doing? Do not the heathen do the same? Be true, just as your heavenly Father is true.*[15]

I prefer the Anchor Bible's translation for a couple of reasons: 1) authors Albright and Mann use the word "misuse" rather than "persecute." We all know how it feels to be used and misused, while the word "persecute" is freighted with a lot of religious baggage; and 2) Albright and Mann use the word "true" rather than "perfect." As a Christian counselor, I can't tell you how many people suffer from unrealistic expectations of being perfect. In this biblical context, the word "true" is preferable. It does not, however, refer to moral perfection but to truth and sincerity. Again, we can relate to being true—true to our word, true joy, and even true grit. We can't relate to being perfect, nor does God expect it from us. After all that's who Jesus came to save—us sinners. Let us consider Matt. 9:9-13, ESV:

> *As Jesus passed on from there, he saw a man called Matthew sitting at the tax booth, and he said to him, "Follow me." And he rose and followed him.*

And as Jesus reclined at table in the house, behold, many tax collectors and sinners came and were reclining with Jesus and his disciples. And when the Pharisees saw this, they said to his disciples, "Why does your teacher eat with tax collectors and sinners?" But when he heard it, he said, "Those who are well have no need of a physician, but those who are sick. Go and learn what this means: 'I desire mercy, and not sacrifice.' For I came not to call the righteous, but sinners."

Aside from reading about Matthew's call to be a disciple, let's pay attention to what Jesus says about tax collectors, who were considered in Jesus's day as unrepentant sinners. Tax collectors were people that everybody truly hated. They were considered the enemies of all. They were traitors serving Rome while gouging fellow Jews. Jesus is saying that even if everyone else considers a person an enemy, Christians are called to treat them with steadfast lovingkindness. Treating others fairly and with respect is an indication of living faith, shouting hope, and loving others.

Jesus also expands and elaborates on the Old Testament scripture of Leviticus 19:18, CEB: "You must not take revenge nor hold a grudge against any of your people; instead, you must love your neighbor as yourself; I am the Lord." Jesus notoriously rephrases this into what we call the Golden Rule: "So in everything, do to others what you would have them do to you, for this sums up the Law and the Prophets" (Matt. 7:12, NIV).

Loving Your Enemies on the Job

By loving our enemies, we live out God's instruction concerning the ways we handle our disagreements and mistreatment at the hands of others. Loving one's enemies does not mean that we magically start feeling warm and fuzzy about them, but it does mean that we humbly show our enemies grace, kindness, and mercy. It means we treat them as we want to be treated.

Marion[16] knew how to make things happen at her job. She also was liked and respected by her colleagues. But when Adrian began working with Marion's team, that all changed. As it happened, Adrian was in charge of making an important presentation for which she was unprepared and ill-equipped. As time drew closer, Adrian panicked and hid her problems from her boss. Marion and her team took one look at Adrian's face and quickly figured something was wrong. So uninvited, they came to the rescue and helped Adrian best they could, providing last-minute fixes. Adrian said she was happy, and Marion went on to the next thing. However despite being saved from failure, Adrian was secretly furious. How dare Marion step in? So Adrian complained to her manager, minimizing her own ignorance and maximizing Marion's "interference."

As a result, Adrian's manager got angry and accused Marion of unsportsmanlike conduct, not being a team player, and hurting Adrian's feelings. Marion was floored. Marion offered to talk to Adrian to sort things out but was expressly forbidden, making a bad situation worse. From that day on, Adrian declared that she was Marion's enemy.

Despite feeling unfairly treated and surprised by all the hostility, Marion decided she would do what she could to help Adrian. Then the next presentation came around, and Adrian was unprepared and ill-equipped yet again. Finally an hour before the presentation, Adrian sheepishly approached Marion for help. Marion simply smiled and said, "Yes." Marion did right by Adrian.

Murry[17] was promoted to the position he had always dreamed of having. He was now on the executive council as a district manager. Murry had worked hard, having served some difficult clients successfully, and, in his opinion, it was a well-deserved reward. But he knew he would need to keep his district running smoothly. Things were going pretty well when Murry heard that one of his salespeople was in trouble. Then he found out who it was. It was Walt. "Serves him right," Murry thought. "He's had smooth sailing in all his assignments, and it is about time to throw cold water on this guy's ambitions."

The truth was that Walt didn't have any particular ambitions. He was just easygoing. He was one of those people who could sell anything to anybody. Murry, however, was secretly jealous of his colleague and decided, if the opportunity arose, he would move Walt out of his district with a demotion, if possible. Walt sensed animosity between himself and Murry, so when the problem first arose, Walt was slow about asking Murry for help, which, of course, was not forthcoming. The problem escalated, and Walt was sent packing.

Walt knew about Murry's jealousy but had never confronted him about it. He thought the best thing to do was to be successful in his next post and prove Murry wrong. However, Murry decided he would "help" Walt even further, so Murry lied about Walt to the CEO, who believed every negative word. Consequently, when the move was made, it was, indeed, a significant demotion.

Despite Murry's jealousy, Walt made every effort to befriend him. It took years, Murry's own stumbles, and a lot of forgiveness. Walt decided to win over his enemy by "heaping hot coals of kindness on his head" (Prov. 25:22). Finally, they reconciled. But when people act as enemies, there is always collateral damage. In this case, not only was a lot of time and energy wasted, but other people were hurt, and God's kingdom suffered.

Putting Aside Group Loyalties

We are probably all well acquainted with the enduring hostilities between Northern Ireland and the Republic of Ireland. Many, many lives have been lost and property laid to ruin. And while there is currently peace, it would surprise no one if the cycle of violence returned.

In the early 2000s, with the conflict waning, Connor,[18] a British Methodist I know, had an idea. Even though he knew some Irish regarded any Englishman as an enemy and that his being British could prevent his plan from getting a good hearing, he was willing to risk it. So Connor called upon some of his American Christian friends with a proposition: would they help sponsor youth from Northern Ireland and the Republic of Ireland to come to England for a summer retreat? He reasoned that, away from home, perhaps the youth could overcome their prejudices and stereotypes and get to know each other in a different setting. Perhaps old enemies could become new friends. Maybe they could put aside other loyalties and create new ones.

Connor's American friends thought the idea had merit, and to his surprise, there were enough supporters for his plan to work. The following year, the group of youth arrived ready for outdoor adventure. According to Connor, the retreat exceeded all his expectations. No matter where they lived, no matter what the politics, the youth found they had much in common. It was like heaven on earth, so they said.

Then they went home. When I later saw Connor, I asked him if there were any long-lasting results or if everything just returned to normal once the youth went home. He had been so optimistic. He shook his head. Yes, he planned to try again; but once the youth went home, old hatreds began to flare, and former group loyalties reappeared. As individuals, they enjoyed each other's company, but as a member of one faction or another, as soon as they got home, they resumed hostilities. It was sad, but perhaps a spark of hope would survive. Connor was a peacemaker shining his light for God.

Loving Enemies through Forgiveness

Here is another story from Peter Storey, the South African Methodist bishop, who became part of the Truth and Reconciliation Commission when the Botha government and apartheid were finally dismantled.[19]

Peter says that the Truth and Reconciliation Commission saved South Africa from many more years of war. As part of the Commission's process, people who had committed crimes or great injustices came forward. Their pardons were contingent on their confession while facing their victims. There are countless stories of gut-wrenching forgiveness. One day, Peter had a surprise. A young army officer approached and asked to speak with him. Peter easily obliged.

Then the officer said, "I need to seek your forgiveness."

"Why?" asked Peter, "I've never seen you before."

"Yes, that's true, but I've seen you," he replied. "Do you remember those times when you came to Robbin Island to meet with Nelson Mandela?" (Peter had been Nelson's chaplain.)

"Yes, I was there many times," said Peter.

"Do you remember a time when you came with Desmond Tutu?" said the officer.

"Yes." Peter was now feeling a bit uncomfortable with the man's questions.

"Well," the man continued, "the last time you were there, I had orders to kill you."

With that, Peter stepped back. No, he hadn't been aware of the danger, at least not there.

"I was about to do it, but I...I...just couldn't." And he broke down and cried. "I was behind you in the bushes that day. I had you in my sights. It would have been an easy kill shot, but I just couldn't pull the trigger, so I made up some excuse for my superiors. Please...please, forgive me."

Peter was deeply touched by the young man's deep sincerity and openness about what he had almost done.

"But you didn't do it," protested Peter.

"But I could have."

"I forgive you."

This army officer worked for Peter's enemy, and Peter didn't even know it. Peter was designated an enemy not because of who he was but because of who he represented. And ironically, that is what saved him. To the soldier, Peter was a man of God who walked on paths of righteousness. Even if Peter was on the island to minister to an enemy, he was still serving God. The soldier couldn't justify killing a man for that. And Peter couldn't deny giving his forgiveness and offering God's love.

Love Is a Way of Doing

Love in the Bible is much more than a feeling. It entails action, how one behaves toward others. Love is an ethic, a way of living how we ought to live. Jesus calls us to act ethically toward our enemies. Too often, we are swayed only by our feelings. Our heart rules our head when, instead, they need to work together. We are called to love God with our heart, soul, mind, and strength (Matt. 22:37)—in other words, with our entire self. And this love reciprocates by making us whole; our faith, hope, and love are of one piece. Our heart tempers the justice that our principles demand with mercy. But mercy without justice melts into sticky sentimentality. Justice without mercy hardens into legalism.

There is no greater example of a person loving his enemies than Jesus on the cross. Even while being crucified, Jesus loved those who were sworn to protect and defend a corrupt world. Jesus loved more than those soldiers who divided up his few possessions (Matt. 27:35) and nailed him to the cross. Jesus even asked God to forgive them "for they know not what they do," (Luke 23:34, ESV). He also loves those of us who too often act out of ignorance and willful disobedience to God.

Just as the disciples demonstrated an incapacity to grasp Jesus's message heralding the Kingdom of God (Matt. 15:16), we also fail. Jesus's mission was to heal the blind and the sick, whether it be of the body or soul, not out of a sense of sentimentality or legalism, but through his perfect love, the same perfect love he offers to us. By loving those who plotted against him, those who denied him, those who mocked him, and those who killed him, we know that he can love even us, and we know that there is nothing that can separate us from the love of God (Rom. 8:31-39).

Jesus asks nothing of us that he, himself, did not do. But how can we do right by our enemies? Jesus gives us some examples that were poignant in his day and ours.

> *You have heard that it was said, "Eye for eye, and tooth for tooth." But I tell you, do not resist an evil person. If anyone slaps you on the right cheek, turn to them the other cheek also. And if anyone wants to sue you and take your shirt, hand over your coat as well. If anyone forces you to go one mile, go with them two miles. Give to the one who asks you, and do not turn away from the one who wants to borrow from you.*
>
> **Matt. 5:38-42 (NIV)**

Following these verses, Jesus teaches us how to love our enemies. In other words, these actions are summed up as ways we should treat enemies. They define what it means to do right by our enemies.

Jesus is not saying to get even or take vengeance on your enemy even if the law says you can. After all, the admonition, "Eye for eye, and tooth for tooth," was a quote from Exodus 21:24. It was law. What Jesus is advocating is much more difficult and it fulfills the intent and spirit of the law. When we strike back, we may vent our anger, which feels good in the moment, but that doesn't make it right and is certainly not productive in the long run. And Jesus is not saying that we let our enemies bully us into submission, for that is not ethical either. Here are some of Jesus's examples as found in Matthew 5:38-42.

Turn the other cheek. When a right-handed person slaps another with an open palm, the blow will land on the person's left cheek. Jesus says that when someone slaps you, let him also slap you with the back of his hand on the other—your right—cheek. In other words, let him slap you both ways—with an open palm and with the back of his hand. In the time of Jesus, and even today in the Holy Land, backhanding another person is a most egregious insult. When a person strikes you, show everyone that the person who hit you is the kind of person who freely insults others, thereby shaming the aggressor and showing your enemy that you are a person of dignity and worth. While their anger might not be defused by your unexpected act, it will surprise them.

Give your shirt. While we understand "giving the shirt off your back," the reference to being sued over clothing is puzzling (Matthew 5:40). Perhaps this refers to case law during the time of Jesus about seeking revenge. A would-be borrower seeks a loan from his neighbor but is denied, perhaps unfairly. But let's say the person who refused to give the loan asks the would-be borrower to borrow a garment in return. The would-be borrower is not to seek revenge and deny the request but to grant it, saying, "Here it is. I am not like you who refused me in my time of need." Jesus is saying, "Give to those who refuse to help you. Help them in their time of need even if they wouldn't help you."

Go the extra mile. During the time of Jesus, Romans occupied Judea and the surrounding territories. Where Romans did not rule directly, their practice was to set up and allow their puppets to govern, such as Herod Antipas, who ruled Galilee at Rome's pleasure. Galilee was a hotbed of rebellion, which had to be put down more than once by the Roman army. In 4 BC, the Roman general Varus lined the road from Sepphoris—the city located just over the hill from Nazareth—with two thousand crucified Jewish rebels. Jesus may be referring to this event when teaching the crowd in Luke 13:1-2, or he might be referencing an uprising viciously put down by Pontius Pilate and later recorded by the Jewish historian Josephus. As it happened, Pilate wanted to build an aqueduct for Jerusalem, and to fund the project, he used money from the Temple treasury.

> So he [Pilate] bid the Jews himself go away; but they boldly casting reproaches upon him, he gave the soldiers that signal which had been beforehand agreed on; who laid upon them much greater blows than Pilate had commanded them, and equally punished those that were

> *tumultuous, and those that were not; nor did they spare them in the least: and since the people were unarmed, and were caught by men prepared for what they were about, there were a great number of them slain by this means, and others of them ran away wounded. And thus an end was put to this sedition."*
>
> **Josephus, *Antiquities of the Jews,* book 18, chapter 3, verse 2**

It is quite possible that many of the Jews who were killed were Galileans. All to say that there was plenty of reason to hate the Romans.

It is clear to us, as it would have been to the crowds that gathered around Jesus, that Romans were their enemies. It was also well known that any Roman soldier could force a Jew into service and use him as a beast of burden to carry a load. We see this when Simon the Cyrene was commanded to carry Jesus's cross in Matthew 26:32. But there was a limit: one mile. A Roman could only command you to go so far. So, when Jesus says to offer to go another mile, he is saying you should take the initiative and freely choose to help, demonstrating your freedom to choose. Taking this initiative shows that you are not under the control of your enemy.

Give charitably. Our times are no different than Jesus's. Everything, it often seems, has a price, and the desire for profit rules. But here Jesus says: "Give to those who need a loan, even if they can't afford to give you interest." In other words, don't seek to make a profit off someone else's misery. You might respond by saying that you can't stay in business very long using this philosophy. Jesus is not saying don't be fair; he is saying discern what is truly best: quick profits or long-term gain through your relationships.

For several years, I worked as a loan officer in a credit union. Credit unions have the well-deserved reputation of giving loans for small amounts. At least at that time, credit unions could give loans based solely on a person's good character rather than their credit score. Fred's[20] loan was a case in point. Fred was a straight-up guy who worked in the warehouse. When his mother died, he didn't have money to go to her funeral out of state. I'll never forget how embarrassed he looked as he asked for a loan. Not long before, Fred's credit had been fine, but since his divorce, he'd missed some mortgage payments. He said that he'd already been to the bank, and no one would loan him anything. He was only asking for $250, but even that amount was impossible to justify looking at the numbers on the application.

I went in to talk to my boss, because I thought Fred was a good risk. She agreed and signed off on the loan. Fred agreed to a payroll deduction, and I cut him a check. We knew the credit union would not make anything on the loan, but it was good business. Fred never forgot this kindness.

Conclusion

What is loving our enemies according to Jesus? Treating them with generosity, kindness, goodness, faithfulness, gentleness, patience, and self-control—the fruit of the Spirit. Treating others as we want to be treated. Freely choosing to do right by others even if there is nothing in it for us. We should do what we ought to do, be guided by our hearts and minds, and be held accountable by a faith community.

Reflection Questions

1. How much do you have to dislike someone before you see that person as an enemy?

2. Reflect upon a time when someone you know (or know about) stood on Christian principles and made enemies as a result. Do you think it's true that if you stand for your principles, you will have enemies?

3. Share a time when you or someone you know was lied about or betrayed at work.

4. Share a time when someone went the extra mile for you.

5. How can we do right by our enemies when we are sure they will take advantage of us?

Bringing It Home

1. Make a list of people with whom you've had disagreements. Pray for them daily for two weeks.

2. Practice your hospitality by taking someone out for coffee or hosting a get-together.

3. Who is someone with whom you need to go a second mile? What might you do?

CHAPTER FOUR
Be Generous to a Fault

For where your treasure is, there will your heart be also.

Matt. 6:21 (KJV)

Nothing Says Faith, Hope, and Love Like Generosity

It is no secret that Jesus talked about money a lot, and Matthew 6:21 puts Jesus's view of money and accumulation of possessions in context. But the verse also speaks to the fact that our relationship with money mirrors our relationship with God, who is generous and bestows the greatest treasure: God's presence. Likewise, as Jesus's followers, we are called to be a generous people.[21]

Faithful People Offer Hospitality

Paris and Sue Cotton had been married about fifty years when we met them. They were faithful members of Linden First Church, and I looked forward to eating with them at their house for Sunday dinner. They had no children, so they adopted whatever preacher happened to come to their church. They lived modestly but comfortably, and Sue introduced me to Southern sweet tea and English peas from their garden. From them, I also learned that talking about the garden would always break the ice in a conversation when you had nothing else in common.

Paris loved woodworking, something my husband was keen to learn. Paris had a heated workshop beyond the garden in the back, and he invited Skip to come over anytime. I had already learned that when people said, "Come see us," they were usually just being polite, but Paris sincerely meant it. Paris was a generous soul, so much so that Sue sometimes worried he might give too much away. In both of them, we saw the light of Christ shine warmly as they reached out to us with hospitality.

When the snow storm, which we had been assured was impossible, arrived after Christmas, it was a beautiful sight to behold. The parsonage was equipped with a minimally functioning furnace set under the floor at the foot of the stairs, so we tried to keep warm using the fireplace, even though it still had not been sealed properly. You could just make out the bank across the street through the gap between the living room wall and fireplace. Even without the bitter cold outside, the house was always cold inside. But we had warm coats, gloves, and boots to venture out into the weather, and we walked all over town. There was no traffic. It was so peaceful.

Then we lost electricity.

Another generous family in the church was the Phillips family. Henry Phillips had a good job with the electric company, and he saw to it that we got our power back as quickly as possible. And we were grateful. Yet, the church was unaware that the parsonage was so cold that my fingers turned blue.

As Linden was also our first church, we were inexperienced; but my husband, who was the pastor, had a plan to get the church to heat the parsonage properly. Consequently, when the church trustees or church council met, we hosted them at our house. Skip draped a blanket over the doorway between the living room and the hall. Then he stoked the fire in the fireplace. Oh, yes, much of the firewood we bought—although I think some was donated—was green. As a result, there was a lot of smoke. This made the room borderline warm, and the air was a little hard to breathe. Needless to say, meetings were short; and the next spring, we had storm windows on the first floor and a wood stove. The next spring, we had storm windows on the second floor.

Hopeful People Are Generous

We had a fruitful ministry in Linden and met many colorful and generous people who radiated hope. One was a keen businesswoman named Lola Mae Averitt. Lola Mae was a member of our church, although she didn't come very often. She and her husband owned a general store up the road from town, and she graciously invited me to come on Monday mornings and quilt with a group of ladies who called themselves the Jolly Dozen.

The Jolly Dozen was just that, a dozen or so women from all over the county who convened every Monday morning to quilt. About 6 a.m., Miss Lilly, who was nearly eighty, arrived and helped Lola Mae unroll the quilt frames from the ceiling. Then they would pin the fabric and batting to the webbing and lay the quilt top over that, again securing it with pins. Their patience with me was amazing, and they succeeded in teaching me how to quilt—something I still enjoy.

While quilting became a hobby for me, it was the livelihood for some of the women. I kept the quilts I made, but others needed to sell theirs. It always fascinated me to see what happened when Lola Mae put some of those colorful quilts on the clothesline in front of the store next to the antiques she also sold. City people would stop to admire, and Lola Mae would make sure they paid top dollar for a quilt and maybe an antique or two. She was generous, but business was business. One afternoon, I asked Lola Mae if she would let me look where she kept the antiques, so she led me to what looked like a broken-down shed. I said, "Is this the antique shop?" I'll never forget how she put her hands on her hips and laughed, "Lordy child, yes. But you and I might call it a junk barn. Doesn't matter. City folks love to think they can outsmart an old country woman like me." Then she laughed some more.

The Jolly Dozen were an assortment of mostly older women, but I wasn't the only "foreigner" they invited. There were two others, and we became fast friends.

I often wondered why none of the daughters of these women came, so when I gathered up my courage and asked, they said that their daughters didn't see the point. But I did, and I loved to sew and hear the stories these women told. At the bottom of every story was hope, hope that things would get better, hope that next year's garden would be more plentiful, hope that their children would be prosperous, hope that God's will would prevail.

As they were generous with their patience, they were also generous with their food. When we showed up on Monday, each person brought a covered dish to share. It was well known in the community that Lola Mae served up lunch at noon every Monday. When we broke for lunch, there was always a store filled with people, eating, laughing, comparing notes on their gardens, and telling other adventure stories.

To give you a better picture of the store, let me say that Lola Mae had one of about anything you might want—gum, plastic picnicware, pickles, pork rinds, chips, nails, notebooks, knickknacks of all sorts—and you could get your hunting and fishing licenses there too. Her husband's pride and joy was his ax collection, prominently displayed and mounted close to the ceiling all around the store. He had carefully painted all the handles red and the blades silver, even though the handles were already red and the blades already silver. Then on each blade, he painted the name and dates of each president of the United States in black. While interesting, they were nevertheless difficult to see because of all the other fishing and hunting equipment strung up there like Christmas tinsel.

Lunch was promptly at noon, and all of the Jolly Dozen brought a large portion of food, which was generously served to anyone in the store free of charge. The menu was country cooking at its finest—although we all laughed about the time everybody brought squash casserole, and that was all we ate for lunch that day. These women introduced me to fried pies, two-stick-of-butter peach cobbler, and all kinds of cakes—7-UP cake, Snickers cake, and dump cake. Yes, there were always too many sweets, but I also had the opportunity to try pig brains, squirrel, and groundhog, which Lola Mae had shot earlier that morning. I can't say that I took them up on their offer to sample new foods every time, but I tried to keep an open mind. And of course, in the fall, Lola Mae made apple cider.

Now, I thought I knew something about cider. Growing up in the city, my father would take us to a local orchard every October to buy genuine, homemade cider, and that was what I was expecting. So, when Lola Mae passed around paper cups of cider, I was eager to take some. Then I tasted it and almost spit it out. It was fermented. It was hard cider. As I looked around the quilt, I saw women, who I knew were from churches that forbade drinking, asking for seconds. I sat for a long time trying to figure it out. These teetotaling women were drinking alcohol in the daytime in front of their friends with no shame, guilt, or remorse. I knew I shouldn't say anything, but my curiosity got the better of me. It took me a while to figure out how to ask, but I finally did. Miss Pearl, who belonged to the Church of Christ (because, as she told me, that was the only denomination mentioned in the Bible), said, "Oh honey, it's not liquor, it's cider." And when she figured out what I was really trying to ask, she saved me by adding, "You're thinking of apple juice. This is cider." Case closed.

Not only were these women generous with their hospitality, but they were also generous in caring for and talking about others. Yes, they gossiped, but it was motivated with all the best intent. One Monday, I showed up at my usual time, 9 a.m., only to find all the women discussing something feverishly. Nobody said a word to me as I pulled up to my regular spot. The conversation had something to do with what had happened the Saturday night before. I thought maybe whatever they were talking about was why there was almost nobody at church on Sunday. Later Skip filled in the details. All the churches were empty that Sunday except the one furthest down Main Street.

It seems that on Saturday night, a father decided to drop by his son's home. His son was out of town, and he wanted to make sure his daughter-in-law was all right. When he got closer to the house, he saw the lights on, and then he noticed a red truck in the driveway where his son usually parked his black Buick. Genuinely concerned, he pulled up, turned off his headlights, got out, and quietly opened the unlocked front door. He went in. Then he saw his daughter-in-law in bed with another man.

Everyone had gone to the daughter-in-law's church on Sunday to hear her confess. It was customary in that church for people to publicly confess their sins, and such a juicy sin deserved a grand audience. That is what the Jolly Dozen discussed the following Monday. As shocked and appalled as I was, in the end, that confession saved their marriage. Everybody knew and simply moved on—because they were generous with their forgiveness too. Who was I to judge? Generosity is an overflowing of goodwill, and most of these people only wanted what was best for the young couple. Still, it's not how we generally think about generosity.

Too Much Generosity

The generosity of the people of Linden, however, was never more evident than when we had our first child. They showered the baby and us with gifts and love. But there was one instance when their generosity was a little too much. The Sunday after Kristin was born on Thursday was to be a pulpit exchange, but I was still in the hospital. The guest preacher was actually Skip's cousin, David, and we had been looking forward to being with him in our home. Skip was scheduled to preach at his cousin's church in a couple of weeks. Before we left for the hospital on Wednesday, I had made sure everything was ready for our guest—just in case. The house was clean, and there was food in the refrigerator.

After David left on Sunday and we got home on Tuesday, I could tell something wasn't right. Things were not as I left them, and I thought it was odd because David would have no reason to make those changes. But I had a new baby, so I didn't have time to think more about it until one of my friends at the church let something slip. As it turned out, the ladies of the church came into my house on Friday morning to make sure all was ready for the guest preacher. They did it without permission, and frankly, they didn't want me to know about it. I was furious and said to my friend, "Well, did you find everything in order? Did you have to clean anything?!" And she sheepishly shook her head and said, "There wasn't anything for us to do." If they had offered when I really needed help or had even asked, I might not have been so upset—but to think that they got the key and came into our home uninvited, even with the best of intentions. In their minds, they were being generous; but it took me a while to see that. Generosity must be given with gracious intent, but the giver must also know enough about the recipient that the gift can be received with gratitude.

Our church in Linden stands out because it was there that so many things happened for the first time. It was there that I learned many new lessons, things you can never learn in school, only "on the job." I was fresh out of school, so I had a lot to learn. One afternoon, Skip came home. Patrolmen had picked up four kids. The two girls were underage runaways but insisted they were over eighteen. It was clear they were not, but the sheriff had no place to put them. The social worker asked if they could stay with us until he notified their parents, and then they would go home whether they liked it or not.

Skip immediately said yes, not thinking that it might be a problem. When he told me about it, I was not happy that he had made this decision without consulting me, but I agreed I would have said yes anyway.

The two girls lied to us at every opportunity. Finally, one admitted she was fourteen and gave us the phone number of her parents. The other girl kept to her story and left a few days later. Looking back, Skip and I made some mistakes, but we were trying to live out our faith and principles. That was fine for us, but it didn't seem to make any impression on either girl. Perhaps we planted seeds—I can only hope. That's the thing about generosity, you can never know for sure what will happen as a result, especially since I later discovered that they rifled through our belongings and stole from us. My things were of little consequence, but I didn't have money to replace them, and I felt anger at their ingratitude for our generosity. That was a difficult lesson.

Because the second girl had admitted her real name and gave us her parents' contact information, we thought perhaps we had done something worthwhile. Skip made arrangements, and we bought her a bus ticket with a promise from the parents that they would reimburse us.

They never did. They lied to us too. What chance did their daughter have?

Linden is on the road between Nashville and Memphis, and hitchhikers who didn't want to travel on the interstate often came our way, looking for a free meal. It didn't take long before we noticed most hitchhikers stopped by our house on Wednesday nights. This was the potluck dinner night at the church, and we fed them well. One summer evening, however, a man stopped at our door, which, as I may have mentioned, was right next to the church. He needed a meal, but there was no church dinner that night. Skip had gone out, and I had just put the food away. I invited the man in and served him what we had for dinner. Truthfully, I wasn't the best cook, so the meat was tough. He took a few bites, then spit out the meat and said he wasn't that hungry.

I felt a mixture of anger and relief—actually, it was funny. Here I had served this hitchhiker the best I had, and he left it on the table. He rejected my generosity. Sometimes that happens, but we keep trying!

Loving People Are Generous

God is a gracious giver. When God gives, God does not trample our lives or force God's goodness upon us. God's love is never invasive. We must try to do likewise. Proverbs 22:9 (NIV) says, "The generous will themselves be blessed, for they share their food with the poor." This was certainly the case at Salem Church. We have served many generous churches, but Salem Church was exceptional.

When I was five years old, two teenage French girls visited our home in Indianapolis. They were the daughters of the family my father boarded with while stationed near Paris during World War II. The girls spoke almost no English, and we spoke no French; but somehow, we grew to love them in the short time they were with us. On the last night of their stay, my father arranged a special dinner at the Copper Kettle, a well-known restaurant. Although I had eaten there many times, that night we were served in a private dining area that sparkled with candlelight. It was so beautiful that we all cried and then feasted on the best fried chicken ever made.

A special Christmas dinner that the women of Salem Church hosted rekindled those beautiful memories. Each year Salem lovingly reached out to the shut-ins in the community. Knowing that many would be alone for Christmas, the women of the church went out of their way to make this a night to remember. Skip, Kristin, and I were invited because Skip was the pastor and we were his family. Seated around a long table were elderly and infirm guests. The meal reminded me of the Bible passage where Jesus describes the Kingdom of God as a sumptuous banquet. The table was decked in the finest silver, china, and linen. Like the Copper Kettle years before, the room looked like it had materialized out of a fairy tale. Dessert was followed by gifts, and we sang familiar carols.

This special dinner was a true act of generosity. The church people put forth their best with gracious hearts. They gave warmly with open hands and no thought of reward. Later, I asked one of the women if they did this every year, and she said, "Yes." To them, this dinner was "no big deal." They did not think their generosity was out of the ordinary—it was just something they did—but those they served looked forward to it all year.

"We Would See Jesus"

Salem was known for its generosity, and like all generous churches, it was full of generous people, like Glenn Abernathy. Glenn was a retired engineer who loved organizing mission trips. He was gifted in figuring out logistics and drawing architectural plans that laypeople could follow. He also had an unassuming manner that endeared him to people as well as a quiet patience when dealing with intractable problems and local government officials. He was trustworthy, thorough, and true to his word. Under his leadership, Salem, joined by other churches in the area, sent mission teams to Central and South America. Not only did Glenn give generously of his time and talent, but who knows how much of his own money he and his family supplied anonymously. Glenn gave with a cheerful heart, and as a result, schools, hospitals, and churches were built. Glenn was living proof that "where your treasure is, there will your heart be also" (Matt. 6:21, KJV).

Many of us hear the words, "It is more blessed to give than to receive," with tired ears, but those who are bounteous in their generosity sow bountifully and reap bountifully, as Paul writes in 2 Corinthians 9:6. Perhaps you, too, have had the privilege of looking into the eyes of a generous person, receiving their gracious gift, and seeing the love and kindness that radiates from them. In people such as this, like the disciples of old, "we would see Jesus."[22]

Conclusion

Living faith, shouting hope, and loving others in this dark world is a life characterized by generosity. We are all works in progress. Generosity must not be invasive on other people's privacy; and at times, it may not be well-received, despite our best intentions. But a generous soul shows what we truly treasure and bears witness to our generous God, who gives us life eternal.

Reflection Questions

1. Reflect upon a time when someone acted generously to you.

2. Share a time when you extended generosity, but it was either rejected or misunderstood.

3. Think of an example of when someone's generosity went overboard, was too much, or was given selfishly for their own reward.

4. How do you feel when you act with generosity?

5. Would you characterize your church as generous? What does a generous church look like?

6. How might you see Jesus in the generous acts of other people?

Bringing It Home

1. Increase your charitable giving.

2. Take some fresh baked goods to a neighbor and/or invite a neighbor for coffee.

LIVE FAITH. SHOUT HOPE. LOVE ONE ANOTHER.

CHAPTER FIVE
Live Like There Is No Tomorrow

Therefore I tell you, do not worry about your life, what you will eat or drink; or about your body, what you will wear. Is not life more than food, and the body more than clothes? Look at the birds of the air; they do not sow or reap or store away in barns, and yet your heavenly Father feeds them. Are you not much more valuable than they? Can any one of you by worrying add a single hour to your life?

Matt. 6:25-27, NIV

Sometimes There Is No Tomorrow

Austin[23] was one of those kids every youth director wants in their church high school group. He readily welcomed new people and was fun to be around. He was also concertmaster of the state youth orchestra. He made friends easily and took his faith seriously. One summer, Austin, his cousin, and his mom made their annual trip to San Diego to visit friends and family. Austin's grandfather had been ill, so the trip had some urgency. His dad had to tie up a few things at work, but he planned to join them later. Austin was enjoying himself, cutting up, and having a great time until, one day, he started complaining about pain in his lower back. His mother found a doctor in the area and made Austin an appointment for a check-up to ensure nothing was wrong. But something was wrong. Terribly wrong. Austin had cancer.

A few days later—still away from home—Austin had surgery. Unfortunately, the doctors could not excise the entire tumor and had to close him up, offering no hope. Refusing to accept the doctors' prognosis, Austin's parents decided to bring him home despite the dangers. It took several weeks and a lot of complex negotiations with the airline, but he made it back. He was transported directly to the medical center where he endured another surgery. Much to everyone's relief and gratitude, the doctors thought they had successfully removed the whole tumor. Unfortunately, what we hoped to be the end of his health scare was only the beginning of Austin's journey with cancer.

In the hospital, he received excellent care and became a favorite patient. Friends at work and church helped in every way imaginable. Austin never gave up, and it wasn't long before he was sleeping back in his own bed and only going to the hospital for periodic checkups. He went back to school and youth group within a few months.

Despite his suffering, Austin's faith never wavered, and he remained the joke-playing, high-spirited guy everyone loved. He'd be out for a while and then return just like he always had before. This pattern went on for about a year. He then went for yet another scan at the hospital, and the news was devastating. The tumor had returned. The doctors kept him, and there would be no coming back home this time. Throughout his ordeal, Austin lived fearlessly like there was no tomorrow—because, for him, there might not be another day. He was not afraid, and he said so. When asked how he could be so positive in light of what was happening to him, he simply said, "With God for me, who can be against me?"

His parents decided to have Austin's funeral at their church. His family and their friends and coworkers, church family, Austin's teachers, nurses, doctors, friends from school, the baseball team, the high school band and orchestra, the neighborhood, and the youth group attended. Some of his friends had never been to a church before. As difficult and sad as it was, the service celebrated Austin's life and witness.

There is more to Austin's story. Austin left a legacy of love and hope. Friends led fundraisers for the American Cancer Society, which were in themselves amazing. Yes, Austin was a brave young man whose life was cut short by a dreaded disease, but he didn't let the disease define him. You could never say Austin was a cancer "victim." Cancer never "had" Austin—because God had him first. Despite the trials and tribulations that came his way, Austin did not despair. Instead, he radiated light. He lived faith, shouted hope, and loved people.

Living life like there is no tomorrow does not mean that we are cavalier or irresponsible in our actions. It means we live fearlessly because, as the hymn goes, "We know who holds tomorrow."[24] But these words can be trite and overused unless we ourselves have witnessed the freedom of faith in another person's life when we need it most.

Free to Live Your Faith

Some church people tend to look at my preacher spouse and me as "professional Christians" and not the Christian professionals we really are. We were both ordained, although I've always worked "beyond the local church." Many church people think because we have worked in and for the church, we are "professional Christians." As any church professional will tell you, people assume that not only is the pastor supposed to be super-religious, but so are the spouse and children—you can ask any preacher's kid. We get labeled because there are unclear lines between pastors' professional lives and their private lives, in part because pastors are always on call 24/7, and to most people, part of our social role is being identifiably Christian.

When people find out that I am a pastor's wife, I've never had anyone say to me, "How wonderful. You must enjoy that!" On the contrary, they usually shake their heads and offer condolences. Then I feel compelled to say, "Oh, it's not that bad." They just assume that being the pastor's family means people infringe on your privacy, gossip about you, and set expectations for you. While there is plenty of that, there is also freedom in not caring too much about what other people think.

When we started in ministry, Skip joined a community civic organization. Every Halloween, this organization hosted a haunted house to raise money for charity. All the volunteers wore costumes, including Skip. He wore a mask, and no one could see his face. As he collected tickets—undercover, as it was—he was surprised to hear how casually some of our church members used rude and foul language. They never talked that way when he was around. And when they later found out who that guy taking tickets was, they were embarrassed and apologized. That was one of the first times we saw that people treated us differently. They wanted to put us in a little box bounded by their unreasonable, ill-conceived notions and expectations as to who we were.

One day while at the post office, I learned that some of my acquaintances were having a party. It struck me as odd, and I wondered why I hadn't heard about it earlier. It turned out that I wasn't invited, so I didn't think any more about it. Only later did I find out the reason. It seems that the hostess was embarrassed to have me at her house because she smoked cigarettes, and she thought I would judge her. Discovering why we weren't invited hurt more than me just thinking they were snobs. This woman thought I was a professional Christian. I just wanted to be me, but she delegated me to the place where she thought I belonged. She judged herself and me more than I ever could. Sadly, her expectations of who she thought I was kept us from really being friends. She hurt herself as well as me. If you live as a Christian who believes there might not be a tomorrow, you don't have to be overly sensitive to the expectations of other people.

Perhaps people treat you in similar ways. They assume they know what you believe and box you in with their expectations. Perhaps when someone sees you angry, she says, "I thought Christians weren't supposed to get angry." Or perhaps you get caught "liberating" a pen from work, and someone says, "And I thought you were a Christian," and then they pocket a handful to take home. While you might not think of yourself as a Christian professional, that is one way to understand our discipleship. We aren't Christian because of who pays us or because of what's in it for us. There are benefits to having a relationship with the God of the universe, and that's what our actions need to communicate more fully. Yes, there is eternal life, but as Christians, we live in God's kingdom now; and where two or more of us are gathered, Jesus promises that God is there too (Matt. 18:20).

Free to Shout Hope

Living as if there is no tomorrow could mean we are free to act as we want, but it's really not true. As American citizens, our freedom has boundaries, laws, rules, taxes, stoplights, and highway lanes. These are there to protect us from each other and make life simpler and more orderly. I remember traveling in Egypt and being grateful that I was on a big tour bus because stoplights seemed only for show. Inhibiting a person's freedom to drive on the wrong side of the road with enforceable traffic laws is a blessing. I'm not talking about these kinds of limitations on our freedom. The freedom we have as Christians means that we don't have to take seriously the restrictions people put on us to make us conform solely to their expectations—limitations that keep us from being who God intends. We are free to live faith, shout hope, and love others, conforming only to God's gracious will for our lives.

Free to Love Others

Living as if there is no tomorrow means that we are free to love those who God puts in our path. We don't have to wait or be held hostage by the judgments of other people. We are free to live a life pleasing to God according to our own conscience, and it means that we accept responsibility for what we think. It does not mean that we live without boundaries or without consideration of others' welfare, but it does mean that we live and love without being controlled by others.

It is also true that Christians interpret God's will in different ways—we have only to witness the vast number of denominations—and being a Christian can help us tolerate differences. In my case, because I have lived in a glass fishbowl as a pastor's spouse for so many years, I try to be sensitive to the way I judge other people, the way I stereotype others, and the unrealistic expectations I put on others. That was why I was so hurt when I wasn't invited to that party. I would never have judged the hostess, least of all for smoking. As the preacher's wife, you can't imagine how many people there were ready to tell me, even in love, how I was supposed to act. Perhaps you've experienced something similar. Perhaps some of your experiences have helped you be especially sensitive to the needs of others.

Free from Worry

Worry is an obstacle to living, period. It robs us of living in the present by being preoccupied with the future. I admit that I worry. There are just so many things that can happen to my children, grandchildren, husband, the economy, the country, the church, me—the list is infinite. Perhaps you worry too. I tried to give up worrying for Lent one year, the time of preparation before Easter, and it helped temporarily. But Jesus offers something better for people like us: "Therefore I tell you, do not worry about your life....Is not life more..." (Matt. 6:25, NIV). Yes, life is more.

There is a lot more to life than worry. Statistics tell us that ninety-six percent of all the things we worry about never happen. Naturally, my first thought is: "But what about that other four percent?" If I pay attention to

God's promises, I must hand my worry over to God. As a mother, I worry about my children. Are they okay? Are they happy? Are they making the right choices? If I'm not careful, I can drive myself crazy. And when I'm on the verge of doing just that, I close my eyes and take a deep breath. I pray and am reminded that my children belong to God, and God has promised to be with them. As my girls grew up, I kept a diary of sorts to record our lives together. The plan was that when they grew up, I'd give it to them as a gift. I gave my older daughter hers after the birth of her first child. After she read it, her response was, "Mom, you sure worried a lot." Oops, that wasn't supposed to show.

Even though I try not to, when I worry about my girls, I do at least three detrimental things. First, I communicate needless anxiety to them. My daughters have gotten especially good at recognizing this, and they tell me to stop—in a nice way, of course. "But I have so much wisdom and experience. I know what can happen," I counter. Then they remind me that expectations shape results. And they do. They are right. We find what we expect to find. Look for trouble, and you'll find it. Worry, and you give too much importance to things you can't do anything about. It's a waste of time.

When I worry, the second thing I communicate is that I don't trust them to make wise decisions. So, here's where the art of parenthood comes into play. Sometimes kids do make poor decisions. But if they're going to learn, they have to live with the repercussions so they will make better decisions next time. "But wait," you say, "You can't just throw kids to the wolves." Yes, sometimes they really do need to be saved from themselves, especially if the consequences are too severe. But even then, sometimes kids have to experience the repercussions of their actions to bring about needed change.

One of our friends had such a kid. Nathan[25] was the kind of child that any parent would worry about because he made one poor decision after another. We were at a church meeting when Nathan was caught smoking weed in the parking lot, but that was just the start. Time and time again, his parents bailed him out. They sent him to camp, therapy, and anything else they thought could help. Then one time, they couldn't save him. Nathan was arrested and spent the night in jail, which he said was the scariest thing that ever happened to him.

Nathan said that, while trying to keep to himself and maintain his tough facade, a very large man walked over and sat down next to him. Nathan said that the hair on the back of his neck stood straight up. The man looked at scrawny little Nathan and asked why he was there. Nathan swallowed hard and told him the truth. "Look, kid," the man said. "I've been in and out of here since before you were born. Look around. You don't look like anyone here. You don't talk like anyone here. You've got a chance. I don't, not anymore. Don't blow it." With that, the man walked away. Nathan finally heard and learned his lesson.

Like most parents, Nathan's parents worried and worried, but they were powerless to control their son's decisions. He had to decide for himself to straighten up his act. When he did, it was still a long road, but that night in the jail was the first meaningful step. We are all concerned for those we care about, but worry is not the same as concern. Worry is a form of anxiety, and the presence of anxiety is never a good thing. Anxiety cuts off foresight, and worry just fools you into thinking you have control of the situation.

Third, worry takes the joy out of your life. You can't joyfully live here and now or anticipate a good tomorrow when you're consumed by worry. Worry condemns you to live in fear, and while you're trying to keep tight control on everything, you miss out. You miss out on other—sometimes better—opportunities. Contrary to what we often think, we cannot imagine or plan for everything. Some things reside outside our control, which can be a good thing.

When our younger daughter, Beth, was six, we moved into a new house. I was so happy because it came with a burglar alarm system. We hadn't lived in the house for a full year when, one late afternoon, I had to run our older daughter, Kristin, over to pick up something from her violin teacher. Beth was watching a favorite TV show and happy to stay home. I went ahead and set the alarm system for "stay at home," because I knew we'd only be gone about twenty minutes. Then Kristin and I left.

When we got back twenty minutes later, the police were at our house. I rushed in to see what horrible thing had happened. Fortunately for everyone, the police officers were laughing. I had set the alarm wrong. Instead of setting it to go off when a door or window opened, I set it to go off if there was any movement in the house. One minute after we left, Beth got up and went into the kitchen, and the alarm went off. The police officers were surprised we didn't hear it because surely it went off before we even got to the corner. No, I was worried about getting back and forth to the violin teacher's house.

Beth, on the other hand, was nonplussed. When she heard the alarm, she ran into her bedroom, got a flashlight as it was about dark, and ran out the back door, reasoning that the burglar would come in the front. Then Beth went to the nearest neighbor's home—a neighbor we had yet to meet. She told him that someone had broken into her house and to please call the police, which he did.

I felt so stupid but was grateful. My little girl did all the right things. She didn't panic. She found help and was perfectly safe. She wasn't anxious, and I marveled at what my first-grader did all on her own. While I didn't leave her home alone for years after that, I had better confidence in her and her decisions, and she did too. I had been so focused and worried about getting one child where she needed to go that I made a serious mistake and created a situation for my other child. To this day, Beth and Kristin are both good under fire, making much of my worry a big waste of time.

Life is more than worry. Worry keeps us focused on the wrong things. Sure, we should take precautions and act wisely, but at some point, we must let go. One afternoon while my grandfather was mowing the grass, he found a little sparrow with a broken wing on the ground. He put it in a box and brought it into the house, knowing that the neighbor's cat would make mincemeat of the bird if she found it. He made a little splint and nursed the bird back to health. My sister and I wanted to keep the bird, but Grandfather said no, it wouldn't be fair. "But what if something happens?" we asked. "Don't worry," he said. So that afternoon, we waved goodbye as the bird flew away. "Will he come back?" we asked. "No," said Grandfather, "He's free and got a lot more living to do." Worry holds us back, and we've got a lot of living to do.

Free from Fear

Living a life that radiates God's love means that we live as if there is no tomorrow, fearlessly enjoying what we have now. But sometimes, life has been so cruel that we begin to fear happiness. We fear that if we are too happy, something bad will happen, and we'll get hurt again. So, we purposely keep ourselves from being too happy. When we are afraid of feeling happy, we run the risk of not feeling much of anything, and we hover in purgatory between being happy and being sad and afraid.

Life had beaten Betty[26] up. Earlier that year, her husband died in a terrible car accident. She and her husband were rear-ended and smashed into the car in front of them. Both Betty and her husband spent months in the hospital. In fact, it looked like Betty would die, but she pulled through. It was her husband who just couldn't heal. He caught an infection and suddenly died a week after they went home. Betty grieved, and just when she was feeling more like her old self, both her parents died. More grief. Would the sun ever come out again? Then Betty's daughter got engaged, but Betty didn't seem happy about it. "What's wrong?" I asked. Betty said, "I'm just afraid that if I'm too happy about the engagement, I'll mess it up and something bad will happen."

While we might think Betty's logic was flawed, many people find themselves in this same position. They are afraid to be happy because something bad might happen or, worse still, they might make it happen. When people are fearful, they often turn inward and begin to believe they are the center of the universe; they often become increasingly egocentric, self-absorbed, and selfish. The remedy? Reach out and serve others. Move away from your own fears and burdens. Find joy and fulfillment in serving others—because only unselfishness can cure selfishness—and that's what Betty did. She volunteered every chance she got. She especially loved rocking babies in the church nursery on Sunday mornings.

One of my favorite stories is about Thelma, a little girl

who suffered from osteomyelitis, a bone disease that affected her left ankle. Because this was in the days before antibiotics, four-year-old Thelma lived in the Children's Hospital for weeks at a time as the doctors tried to get the disease under control. She even had a regular room because she was there so often. She sat on her bed, looking out the window, watching, waiting for her father to come pay the bill for the next week. Then he'd spend a long time visiting her.

But as sick as she was, Thelma was a great comfort to the staff and other patients. She wheeled herself up and down the wards dispensing rolled bandages and saying funny things that only children can say. Needless to say, Thelma was the darling of the hospital, bringing joy wherever she could. When asked how she felt, she just replied that she was having fun. She wasn't worried. She wasn't afraid. No one ever knew how much pain she was in, not even her doctor and especially not her parents. But Thelma found a way to live and serve others even though she had no idea about tomorrow. How do I know? Thelma was my mother.

Conclusion

When we live as if there is no tomorrow, we are free to follow in whatever direction God leads. We will have sorrows and there will be suffering. But despite our woes, we can live unencumbered by worry, fear, and selfishness. We can live without regard to others' expectations that try to box us in. We can follow Jesus and live life without fear, free to reach out to others with goodness and loving service. We are free to live faith, shout hope, and love others. Surely, that is news worth sharing.

Reflection Questions

1. How do people try to box us in with their expectations?

2. When do you worry too much? How would your life be different if you worried less?

3. Share a time when you or someone you know had to trust God.

4. How do you, your small group, and/or your church reach out in loving service?

5. What could help more people be the person God wants them to be?

6. What dreams do you have for yourself, your family, your world?

Bringing It Home

1. Make a "bucket list" of things you want to do before you die.

2. Find something in your house that symbolizes your hope for the future. Share it with a friend.

3. Prayerfully meditate on 1 Corinthians 3:17: "Now the Lord is the Spirit, and where the Spirit of the Lord is, there is freedom."

LIVE FAITH. SHOUT HOPE. LOVE ONE ANOTHER.

CHAPTER SIX
Forgive Seventy-Seven Times

Then Peter came and said to him, "Lord, if another member of the church sins against me, how often should I forgive? As many as seven times?" Jesus said to him, "Not seven times, but I tell you, seventy-seven times.

Matt. 18:21-22, NRSV

Living, Loving, Forgiving

How many times should we forgive? Some might say that forgiving anyone once is more than enough, and I imagine Jesus's disciple, Peter, was in that camp. Consequently, when Peter picked what he thought to be an exaggerated number—like seven times—to forgive someone, it must have been, in his mind and most likely ours, an extreme, impossible act. Jesus's response that we should forgive seventy-seven or seventy times seven, depending on which Bible translation you prefer, surely seems unbelievable. And that is the point. To illustrate, Jesus told a story that we call the Parable of the Unforgiving Servant:

For this reason the kingdom of heaven may be compared to a king who wished to settle accounts with his slaves. When he began the reckoning, one who owed him ten thousand talents was brought to him; and, as he could not pay, his lord ordered him to be sold, together with his wife and children and all his possessions, and payment to be made. So the slave fell on his knees before him, saying, "Have patience with me, and I will pay you everything." And out of pity for him, the lord of that slave released him and forgave him the debt. But that same slave, as he went out, came upon one of his fellow slaves who owed him a hundred denarii; and seizing him by the throat, he said, "Pay what you owe." Then his fellow slave fell down and pleaded with him, "Have patience with me, and I will pay you." But he refused; then he went and threw him into prison until he would pay the debt. When his fellow slaves saw what had happened, they were greatly distressed, and they went and reported to their lord all that had taken place. Then his lord summoned him and said to him, "You wicked slave! I forgave you all that debt because you pleaded with me. Should you not have had mercy on your fellow slave, as I had mercy on you?" And in anger his lord handed him over to be tortured until he would pay his entire debt. So my heavenly Father will also do to every one of you, if you do not forgive your brother or sister from your heart.

Matt. 28:21-35 (NRSV)

Forgiving as We Are Forgiven

Jesus is saying that continual forgiveness characterizes God, and it is God's intent that members of God's kingdom should act likewise, just as Jesus taught in the Lord's Prayer.

Our Father in heaven,
  hallowed be your name.
Your kingdom come.
Your will be done,
  on earth as it is in heaven.
Give us this day our daily bread.
And forgive us our debts,
  as we also have forgiven our debtors.
And do not bring us to the time of trial,
  but rescue us from the evil one.

Matt. 6:9-13 (NRSV)

God's will includes God's forgiveness of us and our forgiveness of each other.

Jesus's parable makes another point. The evil servant owed the master more money than he could ever repay. To put it in perspective, in those days, to earn one talent, a workman had to work at least fifteen years. So, ten thousand talents is the equivalent of fifteen-thousand years of labor. In other words, it would take forever to pay off the loan. Ten thousand talents was an unbelievable amount. In contrast, the evil servant wouldn't even forgive his fellow servant's debt of only a hundred denarii.

It is inconceivable that the evil servant would be so unforgiving when he, himself, had borrowed so much. But let's look closer. A day-laborer earned, on average, one denarius per day, so a hundred denarii was not an insignificant amount in the eyes of that laborer; it was a little less than four months' earnings. Think about how much you make in four months. I doubt that you would consider it a trifling amount. In other words, what might seem like a small act of forgiveness to you can be enormous in the eyes of the person you forgive.

The parable invites us to think about what we owe God—everything. So much that it is impossible for us ever to repay God. While we can't pay God back, we do have the ability and capacity to forgive what others owe us. Jesus says, "Believe it. God's forgiveness is beyond imagining." Because we are called to be reflections of God, at least we can forgive others.

When Forgiveness Seems Impossible

Sometimes people's intentions to act kindly and generously backfire. Sometimes people go overboard with their helping and only make things worse. And I am not saying that forgiveness is easy. Sometimes it seems impossible to forgive. But that is also Jesus's point. We can't forgive on our own—only with God's help and only with great difficulty. We may even find that withholding forgiveness hurts only us, because the other person may not even know he has hurt us at all.

Mary Jane[27] was raped by a friend of her mother's boyfriend. She told no one for many years, and she hid her shame and guilt, mistakenly believing the incident was her fault. Still, whenever the news reported on acts of violence against women, emotions were triggered, her wound reopened, and she relived that horrible ordeal.

Finally, Mary Jane had enough. It may hurt, she thought, but she was done letting this one event rule her life. While she may never understand why this happened to her, she wanted to move on, and she knew that forgiveness was the next step.

Mary Jane was discerning. She could not confront the perpetrator because that would be too dangerous. And she did not forget. She continued to avoid things she knew would upset her, not out of fear but now out of self-care. Forgiveness helped her find release from her guilt and shame and helped her find freedom from feeling defined by rape. Forgiveness also enabled her to reach out to others and share her vulnerabilities with trusted friends. Forgiveness is not forgetting, but it does help a person put things into perspective. That is another lesson from Jesus's parable. Keep your relationship with God and with others in perspective.

Lest you believe that forgiveness is only for adults, let me share Beau's story. I met Beau when I worked in a hospital rehabilitation center as a volunteer chaplain. Beau was a strapping eighteen-your-old recovering from a tragic accident. He had been at a friend's house celebrating their high school graduation. It was dark, and always being the class clown, Beau decided it would be funny to run and jump—fully clothed—headlong off the diving board into the backyard swimming pool. Except it wasn't. The pool had yet to be adequately filled with water.

I met Beau was he lay in a hospital bed with a broken neck. The doctors told Beau and his parents that he'd be paralyzed from the neck down for life. The doctors had done all they knew how to do.

Needless to say, Beau was angry, but not about what you might think. He was angry at himself. He said that he felt stupid; but more than that, he felt ashamed. He could not forgive himself. His injury was bad enough, he said, but the pain he was causing his parents, his friends, and his girlfriend made his own grief unbearable. He felt he had let everyone down. All his parents' hopes and dreams had vanished because of his irresponsible actions. As I listened, he kept saying: "How could I have done such a d*** foolish thing? How can I ever forgive myself?" Then he smiled weakly and said: "Who knew I'd be the guy who didn't look before he leaped?"

Part of Beau's physical therapy involved making trips back to the rehab center, so I often saw him during the following year. Beau confided that more than once that he thought about ending his life. Then he'd laugh and say that he just couldn't figure out a way to do it given his paralysis. It was nearing Christmas—nineteen months since his accident—when once again, I saw Beau. Yes, he was still paralyzed but he looked better, healthier. I was curious, so asked him if something had happened. Had he gotten some good news?

Beau shook his head and glanced to make sure no one

else was listening. "Hey," he whispered, "I'll tell you a secret."

I leaned in closer.

"Forgiveness works miracles."

"What do you mean?" I asked.

"I mean that I've finally started to forgive myself for what happened."

I smiled, tears welling up.

Cutting his eyes to my chaplain's nametag, he continued, "Since you work for God, you'll be interested in this. I started praying again. It helps." He looked at the floor and added, "God helped me forgive myself, and after I forgave myself, I relaxed. I just relaxed." Looking at me straight in the eye, he continued, "There's less stress now. The doctor says, I'm healing better too, and my physical therapy has turned a corner. Sure, I may never walk again, but suddenly I'm not as bothered by the little things that bothered me before. When I told Mom, she threw her arms around me and we both cried. Then we laughed. That hasn't happened in a long time. It felt good."

Forgiveness had once seemed impossible for Beau. Now it was helping him recover a life worth living.

Forgiveness Is not Forgetting

Several years ago, our home was robbed. Anyone to whom that has happened can relate to the feelings of fear and intrusion. I may forgive the robbers for what they did; but I did not forget, and we invested in a security system. Knowing how many times I needed to forgive or remembering that God has forgiven me did not prevent me from taking steps to protect my home and family. I was grateful that no one was home at the time of the break-in, and I thanked God for that. My relationship with God also helped me keep in perspective what had happened. Things can be replaced.

I do not want you to think that I am trivializing forgiveness. Things can be replaced, but people cannot. We know that. We also know that people and relationships can be horribly damaged. A small country town was lucky to have a hospital, and local people flocked there to see the only doctor around. One morning, Tina[28] went into labor. It was her first child, and we all knew it was a boy. When the pains were a minute apart, Tina's husband, Edwin, called the doctor, who was just finishing his putt on the seventh green. The doctor thought he'd have plenty of time to finish his game, so he did. He was going to beat par, and, besides, the hospital was just down the road. The doctor, however, did take the time to call ahead and make sure the delivery room was ready.

Tina's labor was progressing quickly, and the baby didn't care about the doctor's golf game. Tina and Edwin made it to the hospital, but only just in time, and the doctor still wasn't there. The nurse and a hospital volunteer got her to the delivery room. They were about to call a state trooper, who they knew who had delivered several roadside babies, when the doctor rushed in. But he was in such a hurry that he did not take the time to change clothes or wash his hands.

Minutes later, a beautiful baby boy announced his arrival. Tina and Edwin cried with joy. But the baby's head was large and tore Tina so much that she was bleeding badly. The doctor did all he could and finally succeeded in stitching her up. Everything seemed all right, but within twenty-four hours, Tina experienced incredible pain, and fever set in. Because the doctor had been careless about sanitizing his hands, Tina's stitches got infected. Thankfully, Tina survived, but she could have no more children. A lawsuit followed.

Tina and Edwin were crushed. Sure, they were happy about having a healthy baby, but they wanted a big family. The grief of giving up that dream, coupled with physical weakness and the normal demands of caring for an infant, sent Tina into a dark depression. She was angry—with good cause—and she fought back, but her inability to forgive nearly destroyed her.

Forgiveness did not come easily, and it didn't help that church people told her that "surely something good will come out of this." Tina and Edwin even stopped coming to church for a while, using the baby as an excuse. As a couple, they finally sought out their pastor for help. They prayed, studied the scripture, and read books about forgiveness. Then one day, Tina and Edwin looked at each other. It was like it was the first time. They laughed. Then they cried. They were ready to move on, but they both knew there was a piece of unfinished business: they had to tell the doctor they forgave him face-to-face.

The doctor suffered from guilt and remorse as well. He knew he was at fault, but he also rationalized that there might have been other contributing factors. After all, it might not have been all his fault. He was angry too. His malpractice insurance rates soared, making it difficult to start over in a new place. Later, when he got an email from Tina and Edwin, he wasn't sure he wanted to see them at all. He consulted his lawyer, who advised against it. The doctor politely replied a few days later that he was too busy to see them, but he was sorry—and he chose his words carefully—for the "hardship" that occurred.

Tina and Edwin were angry. Here they had worked up the strength and willingness to forgive this man, and the doctor didn't have the decency to hear them out or accept their forgiveness. After several more days, they relaxed and decided that it didn't matter if their forgiveness was received; it had been extended. That was good enough. And it was. They were on the road to healing.

Forgiving When It's No One's Fault

One morning, Clemmie[29] was called into her boss's office. When she walked in, she saw the human resources person sitting at the table, and she then knew the ax was about to fall. Sure enough, Clemmie's position was being eliminated. The company had been on the decline for years, and many other employees had already been dismissed. Even so, Clemmie was surprised—but not shocked—to learn that it was her turn. Graciously, the company allowed her to finish out the month if she wanted. While she was under no obligation, Clemmie decided that she would take that time to tidy up her work projects to hand over to her teammates.

As Clemmie tried to concentrate on what her boss and the HR person were saying, she prayed for strength not to cry. After all, losing her job was no reflection on her. There were a lot of good people out of work. Being laid off was no one's fault. At least the HR folks would not throw her out the door and make her come back for her things later. No, they were trying to be humane, so Clemmie decided that she would forgive them and make the most of the time she had left on the job.

She wasn't sure what her boss had expected, but he seemed relieved that Clemmie didn't have a meltdown. After the talk was over, Clemmie returned to her desk and just sat for a few minutes, not knowing what to do next. Should she tell the people in her department herself or did they already know? She glanced at her watch. They were supposed to have a meeting in ten minutes. Before the meeting, her boss poked his head in and suggested that she not go. "So that is when he is going to tell them.

I wonder who else is losing their job today?" Clemmie thought. She continued praying and called her husband.

The next day was both heartening and difficult. People from all over the company came to her saying how sorry they were. After several days of this, Clemmie had enough and went back to work contacting clients, getting her projects ready to hand off, and she started looking for another job. People continued to stop by to express their condolences and frank surprise that she was still there. "You're being so gracious. Why?" Clemmie told them that it was hard but that she had forgiven them and wanted to move on. After all, nobody had died. It really wasn't anyone's fault.

Yes, Clemmie was hurt and angry, but there wasn't anyone with whom to be angry. The economy was bad, and there was a shrinking market for their products. Yet, she forgave the people who made the company's decisions, including those who had decided to let her go.

News of how well Clemmie was taking losing her job reached the ears of the CEO. He invited her out for lunch, and they had a nice conversation. Clemmie didn't expect anything to come of it and nothing did. Just before she walked out the door last time, her boss pulled her aside and asked her why she had been "so nice." Clemmie smiled and said, "I believe in what we do here, and I want to do my part for the company to succeed with or without me."

Conclusion

Forgiveness is a choice we make, and even though we know it is in our best interest, forgiveness is still difficult. While we know that God will help us, forgiveness takes time (sometimes a lot of time) and effort, even in communion with our Lord and Christian friends. Forgiveness may be offered and not received, but it is part of our Christian witness. If we don't want to be held captive to the past and if we want to move forward in life, forgiveness is necessary. Even if we can't "point a finger" at anyone in particular, forgiveness is an act of grace that opens our hearts to all the faith, hope, and love that God has in store for us.

Reflection Questions

1. Share a time when you forgave someone or when someone forgave you.

2. Discuss the differences between forgiving and forgetting.

3. Are some things unforgivable?

4. Why do some people find it easier to forgive than other people?

5. What can help people forgive?

6. How can withholding forgiveness hurt or hold a person back?

Bringing It Home

1. Find a picture or image that says "forgiveness" to you.

2. Pray for those in prison, perhaps on behalf of those who cannot forgive.

3. Consider visiting a local jail or prison.

4. Make a list of people you need to forgive. If appropriate, consider contacting them.

CHAPTER SEVEN
Make a Joyful Noise

His master said to him, "Well done, good and faithful servant. You have been faithful over a little; I will set you over much. Enter into the joy of your master."

Matt. 25:23, ESV

Overflow

We often talk about Jesus looking at others with compassion, loving his disciples, grieving over Jerusalem, and being angry at the money changers in the temple. Jesus was sent to be the light of the world by a gracious God; surely, Jesus was also full of joy. Surely, Jesus could shout joyfully with the best of them. This is how I picture it. Jesus is God in the flesh. This is like saying that infinity, in all its infinite number of dimensions, is collapsed into our four. Think what it's like when an artist closely renders three dimensions into two. Think about what is lost. Now imagine taking the infinite number of dimensions that belong to God and making them into our four.

Perhaps this visual will help. Imagine taking a sixteen-ounce pitcher of golden honey and pouring all of it into an eight-ounce glass. The glass can't contain it; it will overflow. That's how I think of God pouring himself into a human form. Divinity must have overflowed everywhere. Even if people didn't recognize Jesus's divinity, perhaps they saw and experienced his infectious joy.

Have you ever known people so full of God's love and joy that it overflowed, making you joyful too? To live faith, shout hope, and love others, we need joy. One of my most memorable seminary professors is Dr. Gerry Janzen. I took him for several courses, including Hebrew and the books of Genesis and Job. His love of the Bible and the joy he exuded while he taught were palatable and contagious; it made me love those things too. His classes were difficult, and we all studied hard, but it was worth it. We all wanted to enter into the joy of biblical studies.

For some people, joy seems to come naturally. I wish it did for me, but because it doesn't, perhaps I notice other people's joy more often. Yesterday I stopped in the restroom before going into my doctor's office for an appointment. There bending over one of the sinks was the restroom attendant, smiling and singing joyously. I said to her, "It's so good to see someone who's so full of joy." She replied, "I believe in living life to the fullest." She made me smile. I, too, believe in living life to the fullest. Perhaps I need to show it more often.

It's sad that we so often need a reminder to be joyful. We Christians have the greatest gifts imaginable: salvation and eternal life. We have much to be happy about, so it's difficult to reconcile our dire, pessimistic predictions with the future that God promises. God is Lord of the future just as much as God is Lord of today.

Joy Amid Hardship

I once had a client who described Jesus as having a stern face. To her, Jesus was severe in his judgment and strict in his demeanor. One session, out of curiosity, I asked her if she thought Jesus ever told a joke. She recoiled in horror, "Of course not. How could you think that?"

"Don't you think Jesus had a sense of humor?" She'd never considered it, and, in my experience, most people haven't. But a jovial sense of humor is a characteristic of a healthy person. Healthy people laugh with others and are not afraid to laugh at themselves. As for my client, the day she told me a funny story, I knew she was getting better. The day she confessed to me that maybe Jesus did smile, I knew we were about finished with therapy.

In his biography of Winston Churchill, the great prime minister who saw England through World War II, William Manchester tells the story of Robert Somervell, one of Churchill's teachers at Harrow.[30] It might be difficult to believe, but Churchill was a poor student, and he was considered "too slow" to learn Greek or Latin. Consequently, he was placed with other students in a class where teachers hoped that the students would at least "master their own language." As Robert Somervell drilled them on grammar and sentence diagramming, his enthusiasm was infectious. "In the words of Churchill: 'He knew how to do it. He taught it as no one else has ever taught it.'" And because Churchill had Somervell for three terms, Churchill began to see English as a "noble thing." Churchill's fascination with words was kindled, and the rest is history. Somervell's joy overflowed into his most famous student.

Joy in Times of Grief

When my sister and I were in primary school, our mother and father lost two newborn babies in three years. They were full-term and perfect in every way, except their blood type was different from my mother's. Without going into a lot of medical terminology, there was an Rh problem. It was not known then, as it is now, that the blood of the fetus and the mother intermingle to some extent.

Problems can occur when a fetus's blood type is different from the mother's. If the mother and fetus have different blood types, the fetus's blood gets into the mother's bloodstream, resulting in the mother's body producing antibodies. Interestingly enough, this is fine for the first baby with a different blood type. My blood type is the same as my mother's, but my younger sister, unlike our mother, is Rh-negative, which meant that Mother's blood created antibodies, so that when Mother got pregnant again, that baby's blood was incompatible with hers. Mother's antibodies went into the baby's bloodstream and destroyed the baby's red blood cells, resulting in the baby's death. After my sister, my mother's next two babies fit that description, and both died just before birth. There is much more to this, but thankfully, medicine has progressed mightily. Today mothers are given RhoGAM to prevent incompatibility. All this to say that my parents lost two otherwise healthy infants.

As a little girl, I didn't understand what had happened. In fact, I didn't even realize my mother was pregnant. However, these events shaped much of my childhood, but not for the reasons you might expect. Over the years, I asked my mother many questions about what happened. I learned that, despite her grief, Mother was able to find joy. While she was still in the hospital, the doctor asked her to talk with another mother who had miscarried, and Mother was able to offer some comfort. While I thought it odd that a doctor would ask a woman who had experienced this great loss to come to the aid of another woman, he did, and it made Mother feel as though she could help someone else in their time of trial.

Not only that, but it gave my mother comfort and joy to know that her tragedy was instrumental in the research that resulted in RhoGAM so other mothers would not suffer as she did. As part of the research, Mother, my sister, and I went to the medical school in Indianapolis at least a couple of times a year for about three years. Each time, the doctor took blood samples from each of us. This was unpleasant, despite the fancy Band-Aids and suckers they offered. After the ordeal, the doctor also gave us time to wander around the laboratory and examine the assortment of formaldehyde-filled jars. That gave me a love of science and helped set my career path. I am not saying Mother was joyful in her grief, but her grief did not rob her of finding joy even amid her suffering, and her faith became stronger as a result—a faith that she shared with us.

Years later, when I studied various psychologies and psychotherapies, I wondered if she just didn't repress the grief and pain. There was certainly precedent for people doing that, and it would have been understandable. The idea that she could be joyful in the depths of such tragedy was not easy to explain. In fact, some psychologists would say it is impossible. But I believe her joy was genuine—not a knee-jerk reaction to significant loss—because a result of the deaths of her newborn children was a deeper understanding of a loving God. This is not to say that she didn't grieve, only that her grief didn't cripple her and stop her from finding joy.

Joy Amid Uncertainty

When I was diagnosed with breast cancer, needless to say, our world was turned upside down. Even though everything went well, and I made a full recovery, I remember feeling afraid, not because of the possible pain ahead but because of the uncertainty and, frankly, the inconvenience. In those days, before I knew there would be a happy ending, it was difficult for me to be joyful about anything.

I wasn't depressed, but I was anxious. I again saw firsthand how anxiety prevents feelings of happiness and unfettered joy. I felt chained to my circumstance. It was then that I learned that joy was more than a feeling. Yes, I had read it, had heard many sermons preached on the subject, and had even witnessed it in my mother's life, but this was different. This was my time. I learned that being joyful is a decision, and it came to me by being grateful and getting outside of myself, helping others.[31]

When we are hurt, fearful, or sometimes angry, we often draw up and into ourselves. When we feel threatened either by others or ourselves, we react. We might physically bend over, hunching down in a protective posture, thus seeking to protect ourselves from more injury. One client, who I'll call Pam,[32] made an appointment to discuss her recent divorce and ex-husband. As she talked, I couldn't help but notice her posture. She sat with her arms and legs tightly crossed. Her gaze was directed downward as she sat slouched, shoulders slumped. Pam's voice sounded weak and far away, and as we sat facing each other, I wondered in what distant inner world she was.

After several sessions of the same, I remarked on my observations. I said, "Pam, you have a lot to share, but I'm wondering if you're really here with me." Pam brightened a little and looked at me as she said, "You finally noticed." And we both laughed. "What gave it away? My ex-husband never noticed," she continued. I did notice she was speaking a little louder and clenching her fists. All that time, I had wrongly assumed that her demeanor was only because she was hurting. While that was true, there was also rage holding her down. She was not only bracing for another blow, hunched over in a protective mode, she was also holding herself so that her anger wouldn't explode and destroy her or me.

When we withdraw into ourselves, if we stay there long enough, we can become the center of our own universe, making it more difficult to respond to other people's needs or, as it was in Pam's case, her own needs as well. Retreating and protecting ourselves is a good thing to do, and it makes sense when we are under attack. But sometimes, people hold onto their injuries, and then protecting themselves becomes a way of life rather than a necessary respite. Their defensive posture also serves to "hold it together" or "hold it all in," even though letting go would be much more beneficial.

Joy is an antidote to anxiety because it refocuses our attention. While people can decide to be joyful, it won't happen unless they follow it up with action. Joy propels us into the world and seeks out others with whom to share. Joy indicates God's presence, a fruit of the Spirit; it grows out of our relationship with God, but it ripens when it connects us with other people.

Joy Moves Us Forward

When the wise men found baby Jesus with Mary, his mother, they were "overwhelmed with joy" (Matt. 2:10, NRSV). They had finally fulfilled their quest and found the new king. They must have beamed and stopped a while to take it all in. We can't be sure how old Jesus was at that time, whether he was still a "babe wrapped in swaddling clothes," as Luke tells the story, or if he was taking his first steps, which we might infer from Herod's order to kill all the male children under the age of two (Matt. 2:16).

As the wise men show us, joyful people are moved to reach out and offer gifts. It moves them forward. The wise men famously gave Jesus and his family gold, frankincense, and myrrh—precious and extravagant gifts. Their joy overflowed, and the results were tangible. Likewise, when we overflow with joy, we are moved, and the results are real and palpable. Joy is contagious as are its benefits—faith, hope, and love.

Science has known for a long time that certain brain structures, separately and also together as a group, become active when a person experiences joy: the amygdala, which also has a role in memory, the prefrontal cortex right behind your forehead, the hippocampus, which also has a role in memory, and the anterior insular region, which is part of the brain's gray matter.[33] As joy comes from significant relationships, it can also help propel us into seeking deeper, richer relationships. Joy is both a cause and effect. It's part of a positive feedback loop. Joy motivates us and is also the reward, spurring more joy to motivate us further. As Dr. Laurel Mellin says: "We are wired for joy."[34]

Many have pointed out that happiness and joy are not the same, even though in everyday language, we use the words interchangeably. Happiness depends on circumstances that trigger emotions, but joy, while it has many shades of meaning and can overlap with happy feelings, is more. There is a depth to joy that you don't have with happiness.

> *Joy is setting the soul upon the top of a pinnacle; it is the cream of the sincere milk of the Word. Spiritual joy is a sweet and delightful passion, arising from the apprehension and feeling of some good, whereby the soul is supported under present troubles and fenced against future fear.*[35]

If I had to give happiness a color, I would say happiness is bright yellow. Joy, on the other hand, is rich gold.

Joy Amid Suffering

As Jesus suffered on the cross, bystanders heard him cry out, "My God, my God, why have you forsaken me?" (Matt. 27:46, NIV). Many scholars and Bible teachers believe that Jesus, with his last breath, called out to God with the words of Psalm 22. But as the soldiers offered him a sponge with hyssop and vinegar, he must also have thought of Psalm 51.

Purge me with hyssop, and I shall be clean; wash me, and I shall be whiter than snow. Let me hear joy and gladness.

Psalm 51:7-8 (NRSV)

Yes, there can be "joy and gladness" amid suffering. Have you ever truly suffered? We all have trials and tribulations, but nothing wears on us like unbearable pain. Jesus suffered until death released him into God's waiting hands. Jesus's acute pain was unbearable, and chronic pain can be a living hell.

My friend Eddy[36] had several back surgeries and was on his way to stability, but not a full recovery. He was a faithful coworker, so much so that he came to work on a day when the forecast predicted a serious snowstorm. He should not have come to work, but who listens to the weather forecasters? They're wrong most of the time. Right? This day, however, they hit the bull's eye. The snow was piling up, but Eddy couldn't leave because he had to wait for his carpool. He made sure all his coworkers hurried out as fast as possible. The snow moved in so fast that traffic stalled, and the interstates shut down. Everyone was stuck somewhere—and stuck for a long time.

Because of Eddy's last surgery, he wore a back brace and had strict instructions that allowed him to sit up only for brief amounts of time. Now, Eddy was a good patient, but he didn't heed his doctor's advice—and he couldn't heed it when riding in the carpool, especially that day. It took everyone hours to get home, and while five hours in the car doesn't hurt most people, it nearly killed Eddy. It was not just the pain; sitting so long damaged the repair the surgery had meant to correct.

Eddy went on disability leave and never returned to work. Some of us kept up with him through his wife. When I inquired about Eddy, it was never welcome news, even though she said Eddy's spirits were good and that he was okay. One afternoon, a few of us drove out to his house for a visit. Eddy's health was now such that he was bedridden and on constant pain medication. He prepared for our visit by delaying his medicine, which would have rendered him too foggy to have a decent conversation, and conversation was what he craved.

When we spoke with Eddy, he was upbeat, hopeful, despite looking years older and much thinner. He kept telling us how good life was, how good his church was to him, how good we were to visit, and what a good and great God we serve. He was joyful, but I went home and cried because of his suffering. The following day, I asked Eddy's wife if he was indeed that joyful all the time. She said, "Yes, joy has helped him find peace." She was amazed too.

Eddy suffered many years, although some days were better than others. Whenever I visited him, though, he never failed to proclaim God's goodness with a joyful heart.

Joy Cannot Be Contained

In the Old Testament, joy signifies not only an inner feeling, but it also can be an audible or visible expression. The psalmist meant it literally when he said, "Make a joyful noise." Joy is meant to be expressed. When Psalm 51 says, "Restore to me the joy of your salvation," that joy is further described in the next line, "and sustain in me a willing spirit." This means that the joy that saves us also helps us keep a willing spirit. Willing to do what? Willing to be in relationship and covenant with God.

Just as God cannot be contained, neither can joy, which is a sign of God's presence. The joy of God's salvation creates in us clean hearts and right spirits (Ps. 51:10), enabling us to live faith, shout hope, and love others. When those who have strayed from God experience God's joy as it emanates from us, they have the opportunity to turn and return to God (Ps. 51:13). This is the goal of a life that radiates God's light. It's not about glory of self or for self, but for God.

Joy acts as an inner light that people can see in their darkness; it is a flame of love that draws people to its warmth; it is a magnet that attracts others, not only to us but to God. It is a loud shout-out of who God is and who we are called to be, beloved by God who so loved the world that he sent his Son, Jesus, not to condemn the world but that the world might be saved.

Conclusion and Benediction

Living our joy out loud lights a path to see God at work in the world. Joy enlivens our faith, nurtures our hope, and empowers us to love. Joy is a sign that we are living faith, shouting hope, and loving others. It is both cause and effect. For non-Christians, it is illogical and perhaps silly. It is difficult to explain. . .unless you have a relationship with the God of joy, the God of a peace that passes all understanding, the God of creation, our God, Lord of lords, and King of kings.

Do you want to live faith, shout hope, and love others? Then let the fire of God's love propel you to help you keep your word; love your enemies; spark your generosity; and free you to forgive, make a joyful noise, and live in God's eternal Now.

> *Go ye therefore, and teach all nations, baptizing them in the name of the Father, and of the Son, and of the Holy Ghost:*
>
> *Teaching them to observe all things whatsoever I have commanded you: and, lo, I am with you always, even unto the end of the world. Amen.*
>
> **Matt. 28: 19-20, KJV**

Reflection Questions

1. Share a funny story. How are laughter and joy good for the soul?

2. Share a time when you or someone you know overflowed with joy?

3. Think of someone who was joyful amid suffering. What impression did it make on you?

4. Why do bad things happen to good people?

5. The Bible tells us that joy is a fruit of the Spirit. What does this mean?

6. How can you share the joy of your salvation at home, at work, and at church?

Bringing It Home

1. Listen to some music that expresses joy.

2. Surprise someone you know with a present, or send a card to someone you've not seen in a while.

3. If joy was a color, what color would it be? Share your thoughts with a friend or loved one.

4. If living faith, shouting hope, and loving others is a decision and you are in a tough situation right now, try deciding to let the Lord be your strength beginning today.

About the Author

Rev. M. Kathryn Armistead, PhD, is a Nashville-based writer and deacon in The United Methodist Church. Author of several books, she has had a circuitous career path—from therapist to loan officer to editor to publisher to consultant. Currently, she is the Managing Editor of *Methodist Review,* a peer-reviewed, open-access, academic journal. Kathy is a proud wife, mother, and grandmother. She also serves on the Bible Translation and Utilization Advisory Committee (BTU), which operates under the direction of the Friendship Press Board of Directors of the National Council of Churches to provide guidance and counsel on matters related to the New Revised Standard Version Updated Edition of the Bible (NRSV-UE). She'd love to hear from you. You can find her at www.kathyarmistead.com.

Notes

[1] Enid Strict, better known as "The Church Lady," is a recurring character from a series of sketches on the American television show, *Saturday Night Live*, that appeared from 1986 to 1990, and again in 1996, 2000, 2011, and 2016.

[2] Leonard Sweet, *Faithquakes*, (Nashville, TN: Abingdon Press, 1995).

[3] Names and personal details have been changed to protect confidentiality.

[4] Names and personal details have been changed to protect confidentiality.

[5] Names and personal details have been changed to protect confidentiality.

[6] Names and personal details have been changed to protect confidentiality.

[7] For more information about the Walk to Emmaus, go to http://emmaus.upperroom.org/about.

[8] From personal conversation. More about Peter and his son's story can be found is his book, *With God in the Crucible: Preaching Costly Discipleship*, (Nashville, TN: Abingdon Press, 2002). Peter is also W. Ruth and A. Morris Williams Distinguished Professor Emeritus of the Practice of Christian Ministry, Duke Divinity School.

[9] For recent statistics about church attendance in America, see Gallup's research at: https://news.gallup.com/poll/341963/church-membership-falls-below-majority-first-time.aspx, assessed 9/3/21.

[10] This story is adapted from a sermon illustration told by Bishop Robert Spain.

[11] Names and personal details have been changed to protect confidentiality.

[12] Names and details have been changed to protect confidentiality. This story comes from personal conversation.

[13] Letter to Melanchthon, August 1, 1521, American Edition, *Luther's Works*, vol. 48, pp. 281–82. http://www.scrollpublishing.com/store/Luther-Sin-Boldly.html, accessed 9/4/21.

[14] For more see E. Stanley Jones, *The Divine Yes*, (Nashville, TN: Abingdon Press, 1975).

[15] W. F. Albright and C. S. Mann, *Anchor Bible:* Matthew, (New York: Double Day Inc., 1971), 71.

[16] Names and personal details have been changed to protect confidentiality.

[17] Names and personal details have been changed to protect confidentiality.

[18] Names and personal details have been changed to protect confidentiality.

[19] Personal conversation. Read more about Peter Storey in his book, *I Beg to Differ: Ministry Amid the Teargas,* (Cape Town, South Africa: Tafelberg Publishers, 2018).

[20] Personal conversation. Read more about Peter Storey in his book, *I Beg to Differ: Ministry Amid the Teargas,* (Cape Town, South Africa: Tafelberg Publishers, 2018).

[21] See also 2 Cor. 9:11 and Acts 20:35.

[22] See John 12:21.

[23] Names and personal details have been changed to protect confidentiality.

[24] A line from the popular hymn "Because He Lives," lyrics by Bill and Gloria Gaither.

[25] Names and personal details have been changed to protect confidentiality.

[26] Names and personal details have been changed to protect confidentiality.

[27] Names and personal details have been changed to protect confidentiality.

[28] Names and personal details have been changed to protect confidentiality.

[29] Names and personal details have been changed to protect confidentiality.

[30] William Manchester, *The Last Lion: Winston Spencer Churchill, Visions of Glory, 1874–1932* (New York: Bantam Books Trade Paperbacks, 1984), 161.

[31] For more, read Rick Hanson's article, "Seven Facts about the Brain that Incline the Mind to Joy," http://www.wisebrain.org/articles/neurodharma/7FactsforJoy.pdf, assessed 9/2/21.

[32] Names and personal details have been changed to protect confidentiality.

[33] https://www.thevisualmd.com/health_centers/wellness/embrace_joy/joy_your_brain. Accessed 9/2/21.

[34] See Laurel Mellin, *Wired for Joy,* (Carlsbad, CA, Hay House: Carlsbad, 2010).

[35] Thomas Watson and Patti M. Hummel in *Glorify God: A Yearlong Collection of Classic Devotional Writings,* (Nashville, TN: Thomas Nelson, 2019), 344.

[36] Names and personal details have been changed to protect confidentiality.

Made in the USA
Las Vegas, NV
15 February 2023

67587720R00090